BOYS BECOMING MEN

'For hundreds of years, societies around the world have used rites of passage to help boys become men. Lowell Sheppard sets out to show how today's parents need to be actively involved in bringing their sons through to maturity – not just to abandon them to get on with it. As the father of a boy, I commend this book to every parent.'
Jonathan Booth, Director, Care for the Family

BOYS BECOMING MEN

Creating Rites of Passage for the 21st century

Lowell Sheppard

First published 2002 by Spring Harvest Publishing Division
and Authentic Lifestyle

08 07 06 05 04 03 02   7 6 5 4 3 2 1

Authentic Lifestyle is an imprint of Authentic Media
PO Box 300, Carlisle, Cumbria CA3 0QS
and PO Box 1047, Waynesboro, GA 30830-2047, USA
www.paternoster-publishing.com

British Library Cataloguing in Publication Data

A catalogue record for this book is available from the British
Library

1-85078-473-6

Cover design by Diane Bainbridge
Printed in Great Britain by Cox and Wyman, Reading

In Memory of Luke

Contents

Author's note

You may find it helpful to be aware of several issues I faced while writing the book. First, I am aware that the constant use of the gender exclusive term 'boy' will grate on some. This book, however, is about boys, and therefore I know no way around the problem of exclusive language. I believe in the equality of male and female, and that neither has the right nor duty to lord it over the other. I also believe that many attributes are human ones, and therefore much of what I write applies to girls as well. However, this book is based on the notion that boys and girls are different and although the concept of a rite of passage applies to both, the type of rite of passage that is appropriate will differ.

Secondly, I believe that a lone parent family can do just as good a job, and in some cases a better one, of bringing up children, as can two parents in a nuclear family. I would be disappointed if anyone read this book and felt they were at a disadvantage because there was only one parent in their home. That is not to say that one adult is enough to raise a child. My point is that some lone parents do a better job of bringing up children, not because they choose to do so on their own, but because they recognise the need to invite other adults from the extended family and the church to have a part in the process. Sometimes parents in nuclear families can view the involvement of grandparents, concerned friends, extended family members and church members as unwanted interference.

Thirdly, as I will explain more fully later, I use interchangeably the phrase 'puberty rite of passage' and its acronym 'PROP'. Finally, this has not been a solo effort. Many people have helped along the way with this book and I owe them thanks: my wife, Kande and sons, Ryan and Mackenzie for their patient support; Greta Sheppard, Gerard Kelly and Kirstie Sobue; fellow writers (Greta is my mother and Gerard and Kirstie are among my closest friends) who scanned my material, gently suggesting ways of conveying a thought or a feeling; Ali Hull, for her editorial skills and patience; Alan Johnson of Spring Harvest; David McKenzie of HOPE International Development Agency; the Soultide Missionary team in Japan of which Kande and I are a part; and the many men who participated in my survey and shared their stories with me.

Introduction

'What's wrong with boys?' The headline in the *Glasgow Herald* echoed the cry of adults throughout the UK.[1] It was the mid-nineties, and for much of the preceding decade, politicians and educators had been concerned about the growing mountain of statistics indicating that something was amiss with boys. Emphasising the statistics were chilling images on television of boys doing bad things and these images penetrated our homes, pierced our hearts, and added fuel and relevance to public discussion.

The sight of two pre-teen boys, captured by security cameras, guiding the toddler Jamie Bulger to his death frightened us all. More recently, the premeditated rampage of two teenage boys at Columbine High School in the USA and the subsequent copycat shooting sprees have created collective sadness and worry throughout the western world. Sensationalism? Perhaps, but sadly the truth is that boys have been getting a bad press, and in part it is deserved. Although the horror of teenage murderers, brought alarmingly close by the media, is thankfully rare, scholarly research reveals that most boys are having a hard time. Of particular interest to

researchers are the crime rates and educational performance of boys. Since the *Glasgow Herald* headlined the
question, leaders have referred to underachieving boys
as a 'sink group' and labelled the problem as 'laddism.'[2]
Peter Downes, a former president of the Scottish
Headmasters Association, worried by the comparative
academic trends of boys and girls, noted; 'Boys swagger
… while girls win prizes.'[3] Other UK publications have
joined the debate. *The Economist* referred to boys as
'tomorrow's second sex.'[4]

The concern does not end with boys, it continues into
the general state of men. You have no doubt heard the
old adage 'Boys will be boys.' Usually women use this
statement of resignation, not in reference to their sons,
but rather to their husbands or adult male friends.

In the mid-eighties, I was amused when reading the con-
clusions of a group of researchers who had investigated
whether there was widespread video game addiction
among male adolescents. Those were the days of a revolution in home entertainment. Using primitive cassettes, the
playing of video games like ping-pong and Pac Man was
no longer restricted to seedy video arcades: but could now
be enjoyed in the privacy of one's bedroom. Apparently,
most of the cassettes purchased were for boys rather than
girls, which raised expressions of concern. The report
concluded that there was no evidence of widespread addiction among male adolescents, but that there was cause for
concern over addiction among males between the ages of
twenty-five to forty. The report ended with the question,
'Are some men simply not growing up?'

My amusement, however, soon turned to perplexity
when I asked myself the question, 'Have I grown up?'
I confess that in my darker moments of introspection I
look in the mirror and see a boy. Like the poor lad in the
book, *The Prince and the Pauper*, I sometimes feel a

pretender, a poor boy masquerading as an adult. The fear of exposure is subtle, but gnaws occasionally. I am not alone. Many men cling tenaciously to their adolescence, afraid to make true and lasting commitments. They are Peter Pan wannabes, constantly looking for ways to display their youthfulness. This is not universally true, but, I fear, true enough for a significant number. In preparation for writing this book, I sent surveys to sixty men and straw polled a further few hundred in seminars. I found that the overwhelming majority of them felt or wished they were five to ten years younger than they actually were. Many of them perceived themselves as overgrown adolescents.

> The concept of puberty rites of passage embodies wisdom accrued over many generations.

So what is wrong? I want to offer one possible response. Many strands make up the tapestry of twenty-first century life and the problem that we currently face with boys. Our responses need to be equally diverse and multi-disciplined. My response is just one of many that we should be exploring but is an important one, for it concerns a practice used in bringing up boys for thousands of years; a puberty rite of passage (PROP). Could it be that our boys are not successfully completing their journey to manhood because in the busyness and fragmentation of life, adults are not providing an event that combines risk, ritual and recognition, marking the moment when a boy crosses the line and forever steps into manhood? Is the community of adults neglecting its age-old duty to engage the young – preparing them for, guiding them towards, and welcoming them into adulthood, in a premeditated and caring process?

For some boys, involvement in football clubs, churches, Boy Scouts, Boys Brigade, marching bands or choirs goes some way towards providing such places for interaction, where boys can engage with adults and be mentored by them, but this is by default rather than design. Many men are on a perpetual quest, striving to win the attention and approval of their elders. The father who left the family, the dad who was never present or satisfied, the uncle, friend, teacher or pastor who was idolised but never acted as a mentor may have caused this. The emerging adult may have a driver's licence, a career and even be married, but boyish traits and moods linger.

St Paul wrote, 'When I was child, I talked like a child, I thought like a child, I reasoned like a child. When I became a man, I put childish ways behind me.'[5] Paul knew that he was no longer a child. He walked and talked like a man. Even before his conversion, he took full responsibility. When he became a follower of Jesus Christ, he did so with unreserved passion, not afraid of the commitment or its consequences. The same is not true for many men today.

We need to provide our boys with the certainty that from a certain time, they have 'grown up'. It will take more than a piece of paper certifying that they have graduated, or can drive, or are married, to convince them in their souls that they are men. The inner knowledge that one is 'adult' is simply not there for many. Could it be that this lack of inner belief is absent because many men have never been welcomed into manhood and therefore lack the certainty that they belong to the fraternity of men? Many cultures believe that an organised rite of passage helps a boy become a man. Western industrialised societies seem not to have this conviction. Boys muddle through their adolescence with only their inner compass and the presence of peers to guide them. Peer group mentoring, while having some value, can be a classic case of the blind leading the blind. We need to consider reinventing puberty rites of passage for our young people, as one of the ways in which we bring up boys.

This book, based partly on research gained during my years as a youth worker, flows also from my own experience of growing up and the challenge of bringing up two boys. Boys, I am convinced, have a basic hunger for adventure, belief, ceremony and the active engagement of adults. Meeting these needs will enhance their chances of making the passage from boyhood to manhood successfully. Boys want to grow up and if their families do not help them, they will devise their own ways to prove they are men. This book will attempt, in part, to explore how adults can feed a boy's natural appetite for adventure, belief and ceremony in ways that nourish the growing man within.

Parenting is an art, not a science. It requires imagination, stamina and the help of many others. While we can debate the plethora of theories about male development, one thing is for sure – our boys need our help. We need to recover some of the basics and learn from time-proven practices in bringing up boys.

Each generation, in the words of Christina Hoff Sommers, 'enters society unformed and uncouth.' Sommers, who has done extensive research into the state of mind of the modern boy, contends that in order to survive, society must 'humanise and civilise its children' and when it fails in that mission, it 'fails male children in a uniquely harmful way.' She believes that the 'rise in conduct disorder is one indication that the socialisation of males is increasingly ineffective' and that 'there are now a large number of adults who have defected altogether from the central task of civilising children in their care, leaving them to fend for themselves.'[6]

Her conclusion is a sad indictment of us all! The problem with boys in education became an issue in the 1997 UK election. Estelle Morris, who later became the Education Minister, said, 'If we do not start to address the problems young men and boys are facing, we have no hope.'[7] The good news is there is hope. God, in his magnificent creativity, designed boys with an inherent hunger for risk, ritual and recognition and to recognise a boy's need of these things is the first step towards discovering the keys to successful parenting.

Summary

Something is wrong with boys.

 **Key
Points**

- Crime rates and educational performance are two indicators that have sparked concern at the highest levels of government and society
- Boys are having a hard time growing up, and many adults have abandoned their God-given duty to guide boys from childhood to manhood
- The crisis is just not among boys but also among those men who have never fully said goodbye to their adolescence and are still trying to win the acceptance of other men
- Churches and communities have a vital role to play by providing opportunities that blend adventure, belief and ceremony, enabling the young to have milestones that mark their journey into adulthood – rather than drifting through it with a sense of being lost.

Part One

Why boys need puberty rites of passage

1

Boys and the revolution

You may want to skip Part One if you are eager to get to the practical details of what helps a boy become a man. However, do come back later, for it is here that I seek to contextualise the problem with boys, and introduce the subject of adolescence and a puberty rite of passage. My intention is not simply to inform. I trust that you will be inspired with hope to give parenting your best shot.

Boys are reeling from a revolution that began with the emergence of industrialism and is continuing today as we move from the age of science to the age of spirit. The ongoing revolution is bringing monumental changes. It has touched boys by changing three key relationships: with their fathers, with their families and with girls.

Sons and fathers

Mass production and industrialisation has been particularly destructive to the father / son relationship. Never before in history have boys been as seriously dislocated from their fathers, as they increasingly became in the twentieth century. Particularly for the burgeoning middle classes, it has become rare for a son to follow his father into the same job or profession. Moreover, the historical model of a farm worker father nurturing his son in the time-honoured skills of food production has become unusual, as farms have far fewer workers nowadays. The jobs that many left the land for in heavy industry or mining have also vanished in many communities, along with the communities themselves in many cases.

Boys and families

Not only has the father/son relationship been under pressure but so has the nurturing network of the extended family. The same developments that have driven wedges between fathers and sons have caused an equally dramatic displacement of boys from their extended families. It is true that many parents today rely heavily on their grandparents and even aunts or uncles to help care for the young, particularly since it has become more common for women to work outside the home. However, the trend more and more is towards mobility and change. Many households, in search of career advancement, move far away from their families and settle in new communities. Consequently, many aunts, uncles, cousins and grandparents who have a stake in the lives of children have no meaningful day-to-day involvement with them. Now is an important time for the church to fill the vacuum with a kind of 'nuclear family plus': a concept of family that emphasises the importance of a mother and father but also affirms the involvement of trusted adults in children's lives.

Boys and girls

Several months ago, I was talking to a woman who graduated from Cambridge University. She told me that many of the men her age 'struggle with their image of themselves because they don't want to be "macho" but also don't want to be "feminine" and they don't know how to find a middle ground.' They are caught between wanting to be seen to empower women while being true to their maleness. The behaviour and vocabulary of political correctness is changing almost daily, and while some men are struggling to distance themselves from centuries-old oppressive masculinity, they are not sure what it means to be male in the twenty-first century. Gender stereotyping is frowned upon and the division between what is male and female has become blurred. In many ways this is a good thing, as we are all human and share common aspirations, traits and visions of life. The women's movement has developed a strong and effective voice and bit by bit, the notion of a male-dominated society is eroding although it is nowhere near extinct. Society generally has embraced the concept of equality of the sexes. However, equality does not mean sameness. Despite sharing generic human qualities, the difference between boys and girls is more than their respective functions in procreation and physical shapes. Boys and girls are wired differently, and therefore different approaches may be needed in guiding them to adulthood.

An American book *Between Mothers and Sons* explores the journeys of several women into the world of boys. One mother, who had sent her son to a school run by a women's collective, wrote:

Something about it did not honour his boy
soul. I think it was the absence of physical competition. Boys who clashed or tussled with each
other were separated and counselled by a peace
maker... It finally came to me... I had sent him
there to protect him from the very circuitry and
compulsions that make him what he is. I had
sent him there to protect him from
himself...How could I be a good feminist, a
good pacifist, and a good mother to a stick-
wielding, weapon-generating boy?... A five
year old boy, I learned from reading summaries
of neurological studies... is a beautiful, fierce,
testosterone-drenched, cerebrally asymmetrical
humanoid carefully engineered to move objects
through space, or at very least to watch others
do so.[8]

Robert Bly, a poet who often writes about men,
points out that the 'genetic difference between
men and women amounts to just over three per
cent.' He goes on to say: 'That isn't much.
However, the difference exists in every cell of the
body.'[9]

Public policy in the UK, particularly in education,
has reflected this realisation over the last ten years.
There has been a willingness to experiment with using
different approaches in the education of boys and
girls. For example, David Blunkett, then Education Secretary, in trying to address the concern that
boys were lagging behind in school, encouraged
teachers to find boy-friendly reading materials such
as adventure, sports or horror stories, as well as non-
fiction.[10]

Post-modernism

The revolution we now find ourselves in is substantially different to the industrial revolution that started in the 1800s. The new revolution is subverting the premise on which the industrial revolution took place: science and rationalism. It is the post-modern revolution and brings back to the fore of human concern the twin concepts of spirit and mystery. Boys are growing up in a world where the rigid and rational structures of modernity are crumbling and what is emerging in its place is highly fluid and dynamic.

Overwhelmed? The crisis among boys is so pervasive and powerful that it is easy to despair. I have good news: there is hope! The word 'crisis' has a double-edged meaning. In fact, in the Japanese script 'crisis' is made up of two characters, one is used to convey the meaning of danger and the other is the Japanese concept of opportunity and promise. Danger abounds for boys but, as you read on, I hope that you will gain a sense of the promise-filled opportunities that exist.

The post-modern revolution that welcomed us into the twenty-first century provides us with a great opportunity for families and churches more effectively to help boys become men. Fortunately, the emerging culture is conducive to bringing up boys, for it affirms the human hunger for experience, multi-sensory discovery and things mystical. Post-modern-ity tells us that propositional truth is not enough for human growth; truth has to be felt to be believed. This is good news and one of the areas we can turn to for help is the ancient practice of puberty rites of passage for boys.

PROPs

In this book I seek to reintroduces this neglected practice of puberty rites of passage. A PROP involves the whole family and should involve the whole church. Boys need adults, not only to provide shelter and a safe environment in which to grow up, but also to help them though times of transition and growth. Sadly, most boys do not have mentors to help them understand the turbulence of adolescence or how to navigate the route to adulthood. Left to muddle through on their own, all too often boys only have their peers as guides. Providing a roof, food, and hugs are essential but not enough. It is sad that the practice of letting our young drift through adolescence, with a hands-off policy except in times of crisis, has come to mean that many of our children are growing up confused, ashamed and believing that they are not 'good people'.

For most of the last century, the passing of the baton from one generation to the next was messy, sometimes violent – as we saw in the sixties – and largely ineffective. Each new emerging generation showed distrust and even distaste for the one that had gone before. Phrases such as 'the Generation Gap' emerged as an attempt to describe the phenomenon of generational dislocation.

The fracture between generations can be healed. Adults aiding children in a seamless transition to adulthood can in part, accomplish this. Puberty rites of passage are one of the methods that we can employ to do this. A PROP aims to create a line in time over which a boy crosses from his childhood to manhood. Today, many boys grow physically, but they lack the certainty that they have become men. An individual has an inherent need to know that they have grown up and a PROP provides an opportunity for such certainty.

PROPs need not be gender specific. Girls need them too. I have written with boys in mind but the concept of a rite of passage is relevant to all, for it touches on what it is to be human. We must stop the practice of stumbling from one generation to the next. We should aim for smoother transitions, by more fully engaging with our children as they grow up.

I hope to encourage families and churches to organise puberty rites of passage. Boys need all the help they can get in becoming men and nothing can be lost by rediscovering the role of adventure, belief and ceremony in helping them grow up. The sociological earth under them is shifting continuously and they need added support during key moments of their lives' journeys. A PROP can stabilise a boy, by giving him the needed confidence to keep going, stretching and maturing. I hope that this book will be a catalyst for discussion and innovation in your church and family. If we can create events, big and small, that involve ritual and risk, we will help our children achieve a greater measure of wholeness and inner peace that otherwise is not possible. For we ultimately seek wholeness for our children. There are encouraging trends. For example, there is renewed interest in symbolism and ritual as a parenting tool. But let us go a step further and rediscover the benefits of purposeful adventures and do as parents and societies have done for centuries, fuse them with ceremony and the building of belief. By doing so we will increase the chances of the boys successfully becoming men.

Summary

The world has changed in the last one hundred and fifty years and boys have been left with uncertainty over the

whole process of growing up and what they should
become. However, we have an opportunity created by
the post-modern revolution in society for adults to
rediscover tools in helping boys become men.

 **Key
Points**

- No longer do sons follow in their fathers' footsteps
- Grandparents, aunts, uncles and older cousins
  have less involvement with children than before
  the industrial revolution
- Boys and girls share many common human attributes but are 'wired' differently
- For most of the twentieth century, generations
  lurched from one to the next: smoother transitions
  would be possible if adults were more involved in
  children's passages through adolescence.

Ancient wisdom and 'The Big Impossible'

> 'Anyway, children are a lot of work.'
>
> Dr Scott Peck[11]

Do you remember the film *Dances with Wolves*? It not only introduced Kevin Costner to the masses, but also gave us a glimpse into the fascinating world of the indigenous peoples of North America, particularly the Lakota tribe from the Central Plains. The Lakota tribe, like many other societies around the world, have used PROPS for centuries. They have a wonderfully descriptive term for adolescence: 'The Big Impossible'.[12] The descriptive name is apt, for the goal of manhood can seem out of reach when in the midst of the adolescent years. It is not only the boy who is daunted by the challenge of becoming a man: the parents also dread failure too. The anxiety seems justified. Ironically, at a time when parents, families and communities fear for the future of their boys, society has discarded puberty rites of passage as an aid in overcoming the Big Impossible, despite history showing us they are a proven tool. As we have seen, these days boys are often on their own, tossed about in the deep, turbulent waters of adolescence, vulnerable to the powerful crosscurrents of media pressure and cultural upheaval. Frequently, a boy's only companions on the journey are peers who are as frightened and inexperienced as he is. We can learn from the Lakota tribe. Becoming a man is a great challenge and deserves the engagement of caring adults.

Even though the concept is an ancient one, the term, 'puberty rite of passage' was introduced by anthropologist, Arnold van Gennep, in 1908. In his book published that year called *Rites of Passage*, he describes three stages in a puberty rite of passage:
● Separation (old status)
● Liminality (no clear-cut status, 'betwixt and between')
● Incorporation (new status)[13]

Adolescence and advertising

The term adolescent, created by the same anthropologist who coined the phrase 'rite of passage', is a relatively recent one. It was intended to describe the period in a child's life considered to be a 'safe haven, a period between boyhood and manhood when boys would be sheltered and protected, eased out of the world of toys and books into the world of work and family.'[14] By the mid-century, the term 'teenager' was born, this time in corporate boardrooms as companies sought to identify a new market. Since then young people have been targets of the powerful advertising industry. Daily, if not hourly, teenagers suffer a bombardment of finely crafted messages, fired from sophisticated marketing weapons and aimed at manipulating their values. At the core of every advertiser's strategy is the desire to fuel and define the notion of 'cool.' By playing on their innate desire for independence, media images have stirred millions of adolescents to salivate at the thought of freedom from parental restraint.

> 'Our young men's lives continue to disintegrate at an alarming rate. Since the tide has not turned, we must be missing something. What is it? Do our sons need more government programs, more money, better schools, stricter punishment, enhanced youth ministries, or in-depth coun- selling sessions? Perhaps. However, we find help by looking to other societies, past and present, to discover a powerful secret of individual and national success. This secret is revealed as we study cultures that have long helped their sons' transitions into mature manhood by design rather than default.' Brian Molitor, *A Boy's Passage: Celebrating Your Son's Journey to Maturity*[15]

PROPS from ancient cultures

Puberty rites of passage have been around since ancient times to the present. The Jewish traditions of a Bar Mitzvah for boys and a Bat Mitzvah for girls have been used for centuries to initiate children into religious adulthood. In Roman times, there was an annual festival which would celebrate the coming of age of all those who had turned fourteen. At a certain point during the ceremony, the boy would take off the neck charms that all boys wore, and his clothing, and he would be re-clothed with adult garments and accessories. He would then accompany his father and have his head shaved for the first time. At the end of all this, the boy would be granted all the rights and responsibilities of citizenship. Like the Lakota in North America, many tribes throughout Africa have a moment in a boy's life where he faces a trial. When he succeeds, he is welcomed as a man into the tribe. In West Africa, several tribes have a ceremony for boys that marks the death of their puberty: they are then 'spirited away by older men to an isolated grove deep in the forest. There they are taught the secret lore of the men... When they emerge... they have a new name and a new identity.'[16]

Each of these societies and many more believe that children should not drift into adulthood, but be 'made' into adults, using initiation rites. They believe that a line has to be passed for a boy to become a man. Conversely, if no such line is crossed, they believe the boy's journey into manhood will be impeded. The initiation rite establishes in the boy's psyche and the collective consciousness of his clan that he is no longer a child.

Twentieth century: War as a PROP

Welcoming boys into the company of adults is as varied a practice as it is an ancient one. At the beginning of the modern age, boys may have been initiated into adulthood when they were first allowed to handle the plough, or made their first descent into a mine to work alongside men, or wore long trousers for the first time. However, perhaps the rite that has been the most effective in our society in transforming boys into men has been war. While not advocating war as a tool in the maturing of boys, there is no doubt that the wars of the last century, such as the Boer war, the First World War, the Second World War, as well as the Falklands and the Gulf wars, awakened a sense of duty and responsibility in many young men. Perhaps the only exception to this was the Vietnam War, from which many American men are still recovering. Unlike most other wars, the American soldiers who fought in Vietnam did not come home to a national fanfare. The trappings of bands playing, flags waving and balloons hovering may have been present, but so also was a sense of shame. The soldiers did not return home as national heroes who had achieved distinction in serving their country. Instead, they felt shame for fighting in a war that many of their compatriots felt was immoral. My uncle, on the other hand, while equally traumatised by the horror of the violence he encountered in the trenches of Dieppe over a half a century ago, lived the remaining years of his life with a dignity and a poise that drew the respect of all men and women with whom he came in contact. Although he came home early, suffering from shell shock, he came back to a community and family who were proud of his achievement and considered him a hero.

In many societies, a rite of passage, a ritual or series of events intended to give structure and special meaning to important life transitions, marks the shift from childhood to adulthood. Although the particular content and length of rites of passage differ markedly among cultures, they all share certain common elements. These include separation from society, preparation or instruction from an elder, a transitional ceremony or special set of activities, and re-entry into society with a new social status.

These ceremonies are often public events that herald the contributions to society the young person is expected to make in his or her adult life. (An excerpt from a textbook for teachers.)[17]

PROPs: definitions

Since the terms 'rites of passage' and 'adolescence', and more recently 'teenager', entered our vocabulary in the last century, life on this planet has become faster and increasingly complex. Ironically, just when young people need help more than ever before to enter adulthood, PROPs have disappeared from the sociological landscape. Graduations and birthday celebrations are helpful, but are scattered over several years of a young person's life and each on its own is not a large enough experience to be considered a PROP. Whether organised or unexpected, a PROP helps an adolescent understand the bodily, emotional, mental and social changes that they are going through and helps those around them accept that the child is becoming an adult.

The use of the acronym PROP helps us imagine a puberty rite of passage visually. As we explore together how a rite of passage can help a boy become a man, it will be useful to think visually of PROPs in three ways.

● First, the word 'prop' conjures images of the theatre where ordinary objects help create fantasy. Props in the theatre are temporary and disposable, not intended for everyday use. Their main purpose is to enhance the performance. Whether custom built, or borrowed from the ordinary things of daily life, a prop is invested with something more, something special, something magical. A puberty rite of passage can also create a magic moment, one that will live in the memory of the child and his family. PROPs borrow from the ordinary to create a sense of something larger, something more, something dramatic, something memorable. PROPs are moments of high drama: a multi-sensory experience designed to change not only the child but also the community's view of the young person. The PROP enables the boy and his community to mark a point in time when one of life's corners was turned.

- The word 'prop' is not only a noun but is also a verb, as in 'to prop up something.' Its usage implies the possibility of instability, danger or collapse if the prop was not present. For example, I read recently that the leaning tower of Pisa had to be 'propped up' to prevent it from leaning at a terminal angle, which would cause its destruction. Young vines or tender shoots need to be 'propped up' in order for them to grow to their full potential. A puberty rite of passage acts in the same way. It supports the growth of children, assisting them as they stretch to the sky, and aiding them to reach higher than they could on their own. Buoyancy aids and life preservers have the function of propping people up who might otherwise drown in deep and stormy waters. Similarly, a PROP does not rescue the adolescent from the tempestuous seas of the teenage years, but helps them remain buoyant; greatly increasing the probability of survival as they navigate to the shore of wholeness.

- The third image comes from the world of transportation. Among aircraft and boat enthusiasts, 'prop' is short for propeller. A propeller, of course, propels the craft forward. Without a prop a boat would drift and an aircraft would drop. A prop is essential for a safe and successful journey. I like the idea of providing opportunities that propel young people into their future. A PROP can provide the drive and direction that a boy needs to complete his journey to manhood.

All of these images – a means to make something ordinary into something magical, a buoyancy aid, or a device that provides speed and direction – are helpful in understanding the value of a PROP.

Bonsai Boys

Could it be that, rather than propping up our boys during the intense growing years of adolescence, we have perhaps been guilty of tying them down? The question came to me following a late afternoon bike ride with a friend who is interested in bonsai trees. He is also a talented youth worker and when he speaks of the young, I listen. He explained how the bonsai tree is prevented from maturing naturally. By using high-tension wires and string, the master forces the tree to submit, retarding its growth so that the result is a small, unnatural odd-looking tree. The tree is beautiful, but its attractiveness is partly because of the freakishness of its size. Bonsai is an art form where the artist has full control over a living organism. He seeks to produce a tree that is odd and that will arouse curiosity and interest. My friend suggested that the practice of growing bonsai trees is a metaphor of adolescence in the post-modern world. Every day, boys receive a volatile cocktail made up of media inspired notions of independence and even rebellion mixed with huge amounts of the powerful substance: testosterone. The hormones are God-given and designed to change the boy's body into a man's body. However, the advertisers exploit this natural process and, in a myriad of subtle ways, the media subjugates the adolescent's value system to its own desired end: profit. Instead of becoming independent and free, he becomes increasingly captured by the notions of what is 'cool' presented to him by marketing agencies.

The result: boys, through no fault of their own, are going full speed ahead physically, while simultaneously experiencing the emotional jolts of the media, pulling them this way and that. This not-so-subtle combination works against gradual and healthy development.

Societies have used PROPs through the ages because they believed that a boy does not become a man by default. They would carefully cultivate and nurture the boy's character and values through the use of risk that stretched the boy out of his comfort zones; ritual which ceremonially marked a change; and recognition by the community that the boy was now ready for grown up responsibility and privilege.

In this chapter, I concentrate on the words risk, ritual and recognition to describe the basic elements of a PROP. The values present in those words are also present in the concepts of adventure, belief and ceremony, which we will explore in Part Three.

The genetic clock in boys is always ticking; body hair will grow, voice pitch will drop and reproductive capabilities will develop. However, when all the physiological processes are complete, the boy may look like a man but continue to think like a child. PROPs offer an important aid in equipping boys to live and operate in a world of grown-ups. Something within us all yearns for initiation and passage. If the yearning is unsatisfied, our development is stilted. A PROP allows a boy to be tested and to know, when he has met the challenge, that his accomplishment matters. A PROP is an external event designed to trigger an inner change in the way a boy views himself, his world, and his future. For a boy to become a man, he must think of himself as a man. Many men today, despite having the physical appearance of man, simply do not believe in their hearts that they are men.

PROPs in Scripture

PROPs have been around since biblical times. Many stories in Scripture feature boys discovering the man within through daring escapades. The times were different and it would be wholly unacceptable in today's world to recreate such experiences for our own boys but the stories do provide biblical examples of how the heroes of our faith matured as the result of encountering challenge.

- The life story of David illustrates how physical challenge and solitude can result in successful maturation. His recognition by the adult world came when he triumphed over Goliath. Up to this point, David was just a boy who did not like to hang around with other boys, preferring the company of sheep and the writing of poetry.
- Joseph's life teaches us that evil intentions can result in good. His brothers, jealous of his being a 'Daddy's boy', roughed him up, threw him in a well and were going to leave him to die, when an opportunity was presented to make some profit out of their hated brother by selling him to a passing caravan of traders. This unexpected event resulted in the inner transformation of Joseph, leading to his eventual appointment

as the prime minister of Egypt, a position that allowed him to save his family's life.

● Jesus stayed behind in the temple at the age of twelve, learning from and befuddling the theologians. His baptism later in life marked his passage into his ministry (see box below).

Jesus the adolescent

'Every year Jesus' parents travelled to Jerusalem for the Feast of Passover. When he was twelve years old, they went up as they always did for the Feast. When it was over and they left for home, the child Jesus stayed behind in Jerusalem, but his parents didn't know it. Thinking he was somewhere in the company of pilgrims, they journeyed for a whole day and then began looking for him among the relatives and neighbours. When they didn't find him, they went back to Jerusalem looking for him.

The next day they found him in the temple seated among the teachers, listening to them and asking questions. The teachers were all quite taken with him, impressed with the sharpness of his answers. But his parents were not impressed; they were upset and hurt.

His mother said, "Young man, why have you done this to us? Your father and I have been half out of our minds looking for you."

He said, "Why were you looking for me? Didn't you know that I had to be here, dealing with the things of my Father?" But they had no idea what he was talking about.

So he went back to Nazareth with them, and lived obediently with them. His mother held these things dearly, deep within herself. And Jesus matured, growing up in both body and spirit, blessed by both God and people.'[18] (excerpt from *The Message*). Some of the interesting issues arising out of this story are:

- Adolescents are full of surprises.
- Christ's messianic consciousness increased when he went to Jerusalem. He acquired an intense sense of destiny as many children do at this ripe age of self-discovery.
- Adolescents fall between the cracks of adult expectation. It was the custom for the younger children to travel at the front of the convoy with the mothers and the older ones to travel with the fathers in the rear. Probably both Mary and Joseph assumed Jesus was with the other, indicating that there was not a consensus as to whether he was old or young.
- His trip to Jerusalem at the age of twelve was the custom for all twelve year olds in Israel. It was a precursor of the rite of passage that would take place the following year, a 'dress rehearsal', if you like, for his initiation into what was called a 'son of the law' or full membership in the synagogue or what we have come to know as a Bar Mitzvah.
- Youthful idealism overtook Jesus. The decision to stay behind was a clear one to the immature Jesus. The story teaches us that impulsive, immature behaviour is not sin. Immaturity and idealism are part of growing up.
- Jesus returned home with his parents and remained devoted to them and the family for eighteen years until the time he entered public ministry. There is no conflict between loyalty to God and loyalty to family and community.

One PROP or many?

Since Arnold Van Gennep first sought to explain puberty one hundred years ago, the period of adolescence has lengthened. Whilst in other cultures a single PROP is sufficient to mark a boy's passage through puberty, it may not be enough in western, industrialised society. Adolescence is a long wild ride, full of dangers, but we can help make its navigation less threatening for boy and community, by breaking it down into key stages. The PROP should take place as the boy assumes adult responsibility, but there are other times when mini-PROPs would be helpful. Later in the book, I suggest specific ages when organised PROPs and mini-PROPs would be appropriate. But families and churches should have an eye open for the unplanned PROPs that life's crises present us. Bullying at school, the death of a loved one, winning a science competition, something on the news and so on are all good opportunities for learning and development. However, whether there are a series of PROPs or a single one, planned or unexpected, there are certain elements that must be present to make a PROP a PROP.

Effective PROPs weave together risk, ritual and recognition with moral and spiritual development. While frequent organised PROPs are impractical and unnecessary, the elements of a PROP can be embraced in our day-to-day lives. By blending risk, ritual and recognition into our lifestyles, we will enhance the physical, mental, social and spiritual maturation of our children. Physical development will happen naturally but it is critical to stimulate the young person to develop socially and spiritually and this is where the greatest payoff of a PROP can be. A PROP, when lovingly and thoughtfully provided, can facilitate a child encountering God in such a way that his view of self and others matures. The aim of the PROP is not simply to produce a sentimental experience, but for the boy to discover the importance of faith and values that will guide his choices. Embracing God and his love for people will result in an inner transformation. The key is that the adults who provide the PROP experience invest the event with passion, conviction and love.[19]

Risk mixed with ritual and recognition enables intellectual, emotional and spiritual transformation to take place in sync with physiological changes. Of course, the genetic clock ticks relentlessly on bringing physical strength. A PROP, however, can trigger the unlocking of an adolescent's inner strength.

A PROP can be particularly significant in igniting a child's appreciation of his spirituality. Spiritual and social growth unites to hold the being together. Unless a spiritual maturation takes place, disorder will surface in other areas of life. Mircea Eliade, an anthropologist who has spent considerable time studying rites of passage in a variety of cultures, agrees. She says that a PROP 'represents above all the revelation of the sacred ... before initiation, boys do not yet fully share in the human condition precisely because they do not yet have access to the religious life.'[20]

> 'Some cultures – Jewish, Islamic, and others – have preserved initiatory and sacred processes for moving boys into manhood. Aboriginal and Native American traditions and stories are not all lost and may be of great value. While some aspects of our society are at a time of disintegration, all around us are the bits and pieces of wisdom of the many cultures that we come from. We simply have to make our own ways. What will matter most to our boys is that we make the effort.'[21]
>
> Steve Biddulph, author of *Raising Boys*

PROPs are a tested method which communities and families have used throughout the ages to aid in the nurture of children. Sadly, in our modern industrialised world there are no such recognised PROPs, and as a result, many males are unfulfilled as men, and remain stuck in a boyish vision of life. However, it is never too late to grow up. Families and churches can custom design PROPs that will help children face the challenge of the Big Impossible and successfully navigate through adolescence into adulthood.

Summary

A puberty right of passage (PROP) blends adventure and belief with ceremony and has the aim of aiding the physical, mental, social and spiritual maturation of a child.

 Key Points

- Many children are left to drift through adolescence. Any meaningful rite of passage outside of graduation ceremonies and marriage is purely accidental
- There is nothing new about PROPs but it is no longer a widespread practice in industrialised societies
- We can help our young people overcome the Big Impossible of adolescence by providing them with meaningful events that help them and their families accept they are in a new phase of life.

Part Two

The ABC of boys becoming men

1

Adventure

A PROP has three strands; adventure, belief and ceremony. In this section, we will explore the role of each and how, when woven together, they create an opportunity for inner transformation and maturation.

> 'Most rites of passage fall into three main phases: separation, transition, and incorporation. In the separation phase, the participant is taken away from their familiar environment and former role. They enter a very different and sometimes foreign routine that they are forced to adjust to and become familiar with.'[22]

Boys need adventure

Bringing up children can be a nightmare. Every child is different, but each in their own way – some with hesitation and others with abandon – pushes the envelope of experience, boundaries and parental patience. Boys have a natural compulsion to stretch and reach beyond existing physical and intellectual limits. Risk taking is quite normal for adolescents. It is at the times of reaching that there can often be a crisis of confidence. Within every adventure, there is crisis; moments of danger and opportunities. Perhaps this is why crisis and adventure are naturally exhilarating for some.

The dangers can be both inner and outer. Adolescents can 'ignore or greatly underestimate the risks they are taking.'[23] The search for sensation can also lead to antisocial behaviour. Research has found that the adolescent searches for sensation, and that risk taking is common to all cultures. What differs 'is the extent to which adolescents continue to spend their time with adults who act as a counter-force to those tendencies.'[24] If young people are left to create their own adventures, the danger is physical harm or the development of anti-social behaviour. However, where caring and wise adults are involved in a young person's life, the chances of antisocial behaviour are greatly reduced and the possibility of healthy growth is enhanced. In addition to the high of rushing adrenaline, there is also the afterglow of achievement. The old adages of 'nothing ventured, nothing gained', or 'no pain no gain', are simple and crude, but convey an important truth. This is why adventure is the cornerstone of a PROP. Our society provides many opportunities for fun-filled adventures; such as theme parks, sports, cinematic thrills or virtual reality games. Many parents, knowing of their child's hunger for thrill will encourage them to satisfy their appetite in those safe environments. However, these adventures are sanitised, artificial and meaningless. What boys need are adventures with purpose.

When asked about the attraction of risk-taking, one seventeen year old wrote: 'What's appealing? I think growth – inner growth. And a feeling of independence and maturity in trying something new. Even if I fail, I still kind of pat myself on the back and say "Hey, you tried it, and no one can blame you for sitting back and not participating." I want to be a participant.'[25]

The use of adventure is not only a theory borrowed from other cultures: many youth, education and management training organisations use 'Adventure Therapy' as means of personal development.[26] Much research exists showing the benefits of exposing young people to reasonable risk. Boys seem to respond particularly well to this form of treatment.

A PROP, like every adventure, should involve lots of sweat and risk. There are three reasons why this is necessary. The first is to help the boy learn humility by accepting his frailty and shedding his 'infantile grandiosity'. Secondly, he needs to acquire an appreciation for perseverance. Thirdly, risk can open a door to a spiritual experience.

Instilling humility

Adolescent boys can sometimes display infuriating cockiness. Many professionals call this adolescent trait 'infantile grandiosity.' Boys carry the condition into adolescence from their early years. From the time in the womb through the toddler and into the primary years, a child is accustomed to being spoon-fed and having every need met.[27] While pampering and protection are necessary in the younger years, it is dangerous for a boy to grow older believing that he is entitled to such treatment. Most parents successfully deal with this condition long before the boy arrives in his teenage years. However, there can be traces of it in even the best of boys. By the early teenage years,

innocence can give way to arrogance and even lazi-
ness. Some families find it unbearable, and can
hardly wait for the boy to leave home. One way of
chipping away at any remaining traces of infantile
grandiosity is to provide opportunities for him to
experience the big wild world, where breathtaking
risk and adventure challenge his over-inflated sense
of self. To mature, he must remove himself from the
centre of the universe and understand that he is only
a part of a big world. If this does not happen, the boy
may become a man who has an overly large view of
himself, and a diminished view of the importance
of others.

The road to humility though can be dark and unsett-
ling. St John of the Cross, a monk of long ago, called
such a transformation a 'belly of the whale' experience;
a dark moment of introspection where we are forced to
reflect on our values, resulting in choices and change.[28] A
PROP can stimulate similar reflections and help the boy
turn from a 'super-boy' mentality to one of humility;
appreciating he needs others to succeed. A challenge can
provoke a boy to ask the soul-searching question: 'Do I
have what it takes to succeed?' It can be terrifying, but it
is in crisis that we grow and develop a mature humility.
When faced with the darkness of our own inadequacy
we have an opportunity to get a glimpse of grace. The
experience may not be entirely pleasant but the rewards
are wonderful. Therefore, a PROP should expose the boy
to risk and danger that is appropriate for his age and
helps him come to terms with his flaws and frailty.
While not advocating the infliction of wounds, it is helpful to affirm meaningful pain. Some pain can destroy the
soul but when we take the energy produced by pain and
direct it towards reflection, learning and repentance, an
emotional and spiritual growth spurt will result.

Learning the value of perseverance

Boys need physical challenges that stretch them beyond their own view of what is possible. They need to learn that the good things come as the result of hard work. They are not entitled to success: they must strive for it. By facing and surpassing their own self-imposed limits, they gain a sense of achievement. This seems to be in direct contradiction to the need to be humbled, but, in fact, it is not. Infantile grandiosity makes us believe we are entitled to success, to love, to acceptance, and to power. To mature, however, the child needs to know the thrill of earned achievement. When being asked to go further than he has gone before, a child will have the opportunity learn the skill of drawing deep on God-given inner resources. Part of this deepening is the discovery of the power of perseverance.

One day, when my eldest son was nine years old, we went mountain biking with a teacher from his school who was experienced in outdoor pursuits. The first hour was spent riding up a steep trail with a series of seven switchbacks or 'S' turns. It was the first time Ryan had attempted such a challenging course and he had to get off his bike several times and walk.

Our friend, who was patiently waiting for us, said to Ryan: 'Your legs are strong enough for you to ride non-stop to the top. But you need to strengthen your mental muscles because the mountain is conquered in your mind, not in your legs.' That kind of mental maturity comes as we exercise the muscles of endurance. A successful PROP will provide the boy with an opportunity to learn the importance of perseverance.

Igniting his spirituality

'The Mystical Moment occurs as often as it does in sport in part because you don't have to have one. You are simply there to have a good time or to pursue a particularly delicious passion, when suddenly – it happens.'

Michael Murphy, author of
The Zone: Transcendent Experience in Sport[29]

Risk and physical exertion form a doorway to spiritual encounter. It is in the darkness, in the dismantling of our inflated sense of self, in perseverance that we become ripe for an encounter with God. My spiritual life has been re-ignited since taking up cycling five years ago. I have discovered that the physiological high that comes with an increased heart rate and greater oxygen in the blood also ignites my spiritual senses. We are not compartmentalised beings – the mind, body and spirit are interconnected. When one is affected, so are the other two. Look at the depression that Elijah suffered when he heard the Queen wanted to kill him in 1 Kings 19. His faith sagged and he ran away in fear for his life. The first thing that God did in response to Elijah's despondency and suicidal prayer was send an angelic courier with instructions to eat and drink. On the strength of that meal, he ran a further marathon into the wilderness where he eventually collapsed in depressed exhaustion. It was in this state that he heard from God. Nothing dramatic; God was not in the great displays of fire, wind or earthquakes, but he came to Elijah in a whisper. With heightened senses, Elijah did not confuse nature's noise with God's voice; he found God in stillness, solitude and exhaustion.

The Nourishing Dark

Roy McCloughry said that to 'become mature, a man must learn about the dark side of life.'[30] Some refer to it as the 'nourishing dark'.[31] It is similar to the darkness that Jonah experienced in the belly of the whale, for it is often in the dark that we meet God. As we come face to face with our own frailty, mortality and weakness, we find the source of divine strength. The death of my first son was a rite of passage that life unexpectedly presented me. I grew up as I powerlessly watched his struggle to breathe and I matured in the emotional and intellectual pain that flooded my soul after his death. The experience and its unanswered questions left me less dogmatic and more appreciative of mystery. Surprised by the ferocity of raw emotion that had sprung from my deepest parts, I came face to face with my own frailty and powerlessness. During one of my darkest hours while Luke was barely hanging on to life, an older man, a spiritual man, a down to earth Black Country man, said something to me that brought a trace of light and insight. I have never forgotten it.

> You know, Lowell, the man who wrote the Psalms spoke of 'living under the shadow of his wings.' Sometimes being close to God means you are on his dark side, but be assured that despite the darkness, he is very near.

I had never before considered the notion that God had a dark, mysterious side, that darkness is not always synonymous with evil. Quite the opposite; for it is when we are in the shadows, when life's events are mysterious and we grope to find our way that God is near, intimately near. God's dark side nourishes us.

For it is in the dark moments of life when we can discover more of God's love and intimacy. My mother also taught me a lesson when our son died. She describes the ordeal as her 'oil and vinegar' experience. She wrote these words to us later: 'Like oil and vinegar, peace and pain are twins. When mixed together, the oil always rises to the top. Oil symbolises peace and vinegar speaks of pain. Separately they are hard to swallow, but together they are palatable, as in Italian dressing.'

Kathleen Norris, in her popular book *The Cloister Walk*, tells of her own experience of the 'dark night of the soul' and the advice her doctor gave her: 'Get a spiritual advisor and do physical exercise.'[32] Phil Jackson, the famous basketball coach in America who was also the son of a pastor, discovered long ago that, for him, spirituality and sport interacted with each other.[33] I agree. It is in the time of physical expenditure, the coming face to face with our weaknesses and limitations, and in the glow of hard-sought achievement, that we gain greater spiritual sensitivity. It brings us to the threshold of what some spiritual counsellors call sacred space: a place where God can be encountered. Roy McCloughry puts it this way: 'A spiritual journey of any depth has to be about risk taking, rather than risk avoidance ... the wildness of God emanates from the holiness, the "otherness" of God. There is no wildness in the human soul that does not come from the dying embers of the fire that God has placed in every human being.'[34]

'Initiation into a richer, deeper, mature way of being human always occurs in sacred time and space.'

Steven Boyd[35]

Danger, adventure, intense physical exertion, risk, crisis: call it what you like, it is a great way to introduce a child to the realm of the spirit. However, even if a spiritual experience does not take place, the boy will gain a greater sense of confidence in himself and his ability to reach beyond his comfort zones.

My friend Eric Delve, told me of a remarkable adventure he had a month before his thirteenth birthday.

> My mother and father allowed me to do something which I do not think I could allow a twelve year old boy to do today. I set off from my home in Wimbledon at about five p.m. one evening and rode through the night and the following day to arrive in Brixham, two hundred miles away and twenty-three hours later. I calculated that I had spent about eighteen hours in riding at an average speed of about twelve miles per hour. I rode through that night with nothing but the light of a small bicycle lamp to show me the way. When I arrived at Salisbury, I was so cold and tired that I opened the door of a 'Dr Who' type police box and curled up to go to sleep. I was woken up thirty minutes later by a police sergeant who told me that that was not what they were there for and kicked me out.[36]

Eric said the experience 'laid down a kind of emotional marker. From that point on I knew I could survive.' The experience built within him a confidence and self-reliance that no other experience could.

Guidelines for planning the adventure

A puberty rite of passage should mark the point when the boy becomes a man. However, mini-PROPs can be

useful during other periods of a boy's long period of
adolescence. We will explore both kinds in Part Three
and what are the key ages when they would be appropriate. However, no matter whether it is a mini-PROP in
the younger years or a full-fledged PROP in the late
teens, the cornerstone of adventure is crucial to making
the PROP effective. It is critical that the adventure is a
real one, caringly crafted by parents and other adults
working together. Here are some guidelines when planning the adventure and risk-taking for the adolescent:

1 Involve the boy in the planning process

Ensure that your son understands what a rite of passage
is and how it can help him grow and mature. Then ask
him for his ideas as to what adventure or challenge he
thinks would help him learn the principles of perseverance and stretch him beyond his own limits. Ultimately,
he must believe that the challenge is achievable. Remind
him the PROP is meant to be tough, which means it may
not necessarily be fun.

2 Encourage the use of reflective tools

These might include keeping a journal, writing poetry or
simply keeping a log where the basic detail, facts and
figures of his experience are kept. Some boys may find
this off-putting, so you may need to be imaginative in
getting them to do it. For example, you could give them
a palm pilot or a pocket computer of some sort and ask
them to write an email each day to themselves, you or
even an imaginary friend. Or you could suggest 'blogging'[37] a growing internet fad where a journal is kept for
the world to read. Another idea would be a video diary,
for those who are more comfortable with image than

text. The means does not matter, as long as the inner journey is recorded in some way.

3 Bathe the PROP in prayer

Spiritual encounter and adventure are vital to the development of the boy for they enable the adolescent to 'wonder' about God, the cosmos and the meaning of life. Spiritual experience is usually the pivotal point in an initiatory rite where the child can have a glimpse of God and gain a vision of life and the future. It is vital, therefore, that the PROP is bathed in prayer.

4 Do not create expectations but nurture anticipation

We must be careful not to create specific expectations of how or what God will say or do, for this could cause great harm if God chooses a different means of encounter to the one we suggested.

5 Ensure there are moments of solitude

The boy may need to go solo – a night in the tent on his own, a long walk, an afternoon reading or writing poetry, climbing a major hill or small mountain alone – the options are endless.

6 Guarantee safety

The adventure should involve risk, but the risk should be responsibly and in some cases professionally managed. For example, if you are going abseiling, use professionals who will ensure the use of proper equipment and procedures.

7 Set the boy up for success

Choosing the right challenge is critical. It must challenge and stretch while also being within reach.

Summary

Boys have a built-in hunger for adventure. While there are dangers present for the adventure-seeking boy, this natural trait is important in bringing inner transformation.

 Key Points

- The risk element of the PROP challenges the teenager on the importance of humility whilst giving him a lesson in perseverance
- Physical activity, risk and/or crisis can create a heightened state of awareness that can, in turn, open the door to spiritual experience.

Tips

While physical challenge is important, it need not be a sport related activity. However, it should involve physical exertion of some sort, that results in a physiological stimulation (i.e. increased heart rate and increased oxygen in the blood, cleansing of pores through sweat and a sense of physical depletion that stems from the expenditure of energy). It could be a work project, a fast or a marathon walking tour of museums or a mapping of the night sky with a telescope. God's natural wonders are a great tool to help the boy ponder his own smallness and the greatness of God. Why wait? Put the book down, talk to your son, and plan an adventure together.

2

Belief

> Train a child in the way he should go, and when he is old he will not turn from it.
>
> Proverbs 22:6

> Be still, and know that I am God.
>
> Psalm 46:10

I was wrong. Many years ago when arguing that Christianity was reasonable, I would say, 'The quality of one's understanding determines the quality of one's experience'. I was already bordering on post-modern thought by giving experience some validity, but at the same time arrogantly proclaiming that subjective experience had no part in determining truth. In the age of science, feeling was suspect, and certainly not trustworthy in proving anything. This is no longer the state of mind of young people. Now it can be said, 'the quality of experience determines the quality of understanding.' In other words, truth is not truth unless felt. This post-modern phenomenon is not contrary to Christian belief, for God is knowable through head and heart. A PROP provides an experience conducive to learning. In times of pressure, challenge, darkness, exhaustion etc, God becomes relevant. Of course, he is always there, always active, always present, but sometimes he feels intimately near. At our lowest ebb or richest glow, faith can erupt within, bringing an inner sigh, a whisper of worship and our whole being declares, 'God, you are there.' Adventure may be the cornerstone of a PROP, but belief is the foundation on which to build a life. A PROP can help build belief in three things: God, a value system and a purposeful future.

God

Christians want their children to embrace faith in Christ. However, faith comes not simply as the result of mentally accepting a creed, although that can be an important first step. Children will need an experience that validates the truth. Of course, every child is different. Some may lean to a more analytical approach to information while others are more intuitive. Facts do matter. The fact is that Jesus is alive. There was a bodily resurrection. For some, to believe, however, the truth of Jesus has to be 'felt.' A PROP, which is experiential, can awaken spiritual hunger in a child and enable the young person to feel God. The blending of risk with ritual hopefully makes such a moment of faith inevitable.

A warning about doctrine!

No longer are most young people happy to accept what some have called propositional truth. They are suspicious both of set answers as a response to complicated questions and of dogma. Rationalism, on its own, is insufficient for young people to believe. They need to experience truth in order to trust in it. Whether through ritual, metaphor or symbolism, the young today are open to mystery and the supernatural. A successful PROP builds on this disposition, seeking to introduce adolescents to transcendence – to the Creator. They are looking for answers, but the answers must include the subjective as well as the objective. They want to encounter something that is spiritually real through head and heart, and search for peepholes in the realm of the ordinary for glimpses of the mysteries of the universe.

The Bible teaches us that 'without faith it is impossible to please God'.[38] 'What is faith?' some may ask. The answer is worthy of lifelong inquiry and application. Often we turn to metaphors to understand the nature of faith. One metaphor often used is the floor; a place on which we stand. I am not sure this is the best image to use, for it presents faith as static. Faith is not a set of static wooden planks. It is much better to promote faith as a trampoline, which is responsive, giving bounce, thrill and moments of gravity-defying lift. This image of faith is far more attractive to the young, but remains true to Scripture. John Wesley described Christianity as a 'never-ending adventure'.[39] He was right, and we commit sacrilege if we present it as anything less.

Downloading values and wisdom

(Boys) 'need to find answers to big questions, to begin new adventures and challenges, and to learn competencies for living – as their body clock is urging them on.'[40]
Steve Biddulph

A young person's experience of God will not prove to anyone else that God exists but it will be proof to them, and that is what matters. However, a PROP must be more than a mystical momentary belief in the transcendent. Boys need more than a mystical moment; they need to know that belief is relevant to everyday life. They need to embrace a worldview and value system that is rooted in belief, and know that an experience of God makes practical sense in everyday life. The primary trait of Christian behaviour is love. The Bible goes on and on about it, particularly in the New Testament but not in the slushy sentimental fashion of Hollywood or pop music. Boys need to learn that belief in Christ expresses itself through everyday actions of service and compassion. The problem is that many times we can feel we are coming up against a wall of disinterest and even rejection in the values we know to be important. For a parent eager for their child to believe what they believe, it can be exceedingly frustrating.

Youthful arrogance can discourage meaningful communication between parent and child. Usually a conversation either ends up one sided or as an intense argument. However, the fear of rebuff must not cause us to retreat from our responsibility for teaching and guiding our teenagers. A PROP provides a great forum for discussion to take place. It is in this regard that an organised PROP can serve the parent and child well. If properly explained long before the PROP takes place, the child is likely to anticipate the PROP and look forward to learning from his elders. To ensure that they view the upcoming PROP positively make sure that they know four things:

- They are involved in the planning
- It will be a multi-faceted adventure

- They will learn things that will help them understand what it is to be an adult
- The rewards will be greater privilege and respons-ibility.

In understanding a PROP to be these four things, the child will view it as a sort of pre-school for his next phase of development and will be more likely to be eager to soak up all that you teach him.

Dreams of a purposeful future

I like maps. In addition to hard copy maps, I have a navigational system in my car and a global positioning system for my bicycle. In the dense maze of 'look-alike' streets of urban Japan, these instruments have saved me many times from getting lost. Maps are important to me for three reasons:

- I like to know where I am
- I like to know where I am going
- I like to know all the possible options as to how to get from where I am to where I am going.

Many men today do not know where they are going. We celebrate birthdays, graduations, and marriages but many men have never been asked: 'What is your dream? What is your purpose in life?' For men whose passage into adulthood was poorly managed or even thwarted, life is often lived in a kind of 'twilight zone', caught in a chasm between boyhood and manhood; an extended immaturity marked by insecu-rity, changeability and the absence of stability, self-know-ledge and a sense of purpose. Like an aircraft unable to find a place to land, the perpetual adolescent circles endlessly around the concept of adulthood, but never actually touches down. I am not suggesting that a boy should have a blueprint for his life but he needs a compass setting, a point on the horizon for a point of reference when making choices. A PROP enables a young person to think these things through and solidify in his own mind what his life is about and what his ultimate aims are in terms of the kind of person he wants to become.

For centuries, other cultures have believed that boys need to have a vision of the future that was purposeful and benefited the world. One such practice to achieve this is a vision quest. You may have heard of it. It is a rite of passage practised by many aboriginal tribes in North America. Typically, it involves spending time with the elders to learn the ways of the tribe, followed by a time of praying and fasting in the wild. Sometimes the boy is required to stay within a circle of stones until he receives an insight, a vision or a dream about his future and his purpose in life. The young man then returns to his clan and shares what he has seen, and the elders of the village assist him in the interpretation and the application. Often the boy receives a new name that relates to the vision. Some Christians may feel uncomfortable with certain aspects of this pagan practice, which is understandable, for it is rooted in animist theology. However, if we believe that all humans are made in the image of God and that he is the Creator of all things, we can learn from the practices of other cultures, redeem some of their aspects and invest them with Christian meaning. The concept of a Vision Quest is one example of a cultural practice that reflects the need for young people to acquire a sense of purpose of destiny, to have a dream.

A description of a Vision Quest by Black Elk

'A Vision Quest is an experience of deeper under-standing of nature and spirit. It is a ceremony practiced by American Indians. To prepare for this "insight" one must first cleanse the body and mind by going through an Inipi or sweat lodge. Then with the help of a Holy Man, one is told cer-tain things and must go to a spot, usually on a holy mountain, and stay two or three days. During this time no food is eaten and one does not sleep but spends the time in deep prayer and observa-tion. Many times, but not always, there is a vision. This vision is then shared with the Holy Man to help learn its meaning. Sometimes the meaning is not shown for several years afterwards.'[41]

A PROP provides a boy with an opportunity to reflect on the future and the meaning of life. Such reflection can bring an inner transformation. Many men today are lacking in passion and in a sense of purpose. They may be conscientious and hardworking but they are aimless. Perhaps it is because they have never received an answer to life's fundamental questions: 'Who am I and why am I here?' Every human needs to have an inner compass with a clear bearing of their purpose in life. No, not all will become famous, wealthy, or powerful in political terms, but the very fact we are made in the image of God means we are also able to create. Young people need to know that they can change the world, make it a better place and do great things. I do not want to imply, as said earlier, that a boy needs to have a blue-print for his life. God's plan for all of us while we are on earth is to be his representatives, agents of the Kingdom.

The most favourite subject of Jesus was the Kingdom of God. His mission was to inaugurate God's Kingdom on earth. It has started and one day he will come again and complete the job. In the meantime, we are to carry on the work. The Kingdom of God is not some otherworldly state of mind but it involves a friendship with God that has an ethical outworking. Even if there is no shining light or message in the sky, a boy could simply spend time reading passages of Scripture such as the gospels in the New Testament and the Psalms and the Proverbs in the Old Testament, in order to discover what God's will is for his life.

Two adolescent experiences that have propelled me through life

Between the ages of ten and twelve respectively, I had two experiences that instilled within me a sense of destiny. The first was a dream and the second a challenge.

A Dream

When I was ten I dreamt I was in the back garden with a ladder beside me. Suddenly the ladder stood up and, unaided, pointed towards the sky. I climbed the ladder rung by rung. At the top, I saw an image of Christ hovering and beckoning me to join him. I could not see his face because of the brilliance of the light but felt an incredible peace. The next moment we were no longer in my back garden but soaring around the world at incredible speed. When I woke, I was crying and ran into my parents' room. I knew that the dream was spiritual and was a portent of things to come in my life. I have seldom told anyone this story, and was hesitant to write it down for I know that my subjective experience is not a persuasive proof of God. However, it was and still is important to me. I still feel a tingle and sense of affirmation that Christ was interested in me at the age of ten when I recall the dream. It was from then that I began to have a developing love of travel, creation and the world.

A Challenge

The second experience took place two years later. At school, we learned of the poor in Haiti and of a thirty-five mile sponsored walk-a-thon to help them. It was the first time I had really thought about the needs of others, particular those in nations crippled by poverty and debt. I was intrigued with the thought that I could do something about it. So, in May 1967, I joined twenty thousand others and walked thirty-five miles around and through our city of Winnipeg. It was a rite of passage for me. I learned that I could make a difference and I knew that it would not be the last time I did so.

The value of a planned PROP

PROPs and mini-PROPs often happen unexpectedly. They come as one of life's surprises and bring an unanticipated opportunity for learning and growth. The unexpected PROP usually comes in the form of a crisis, such as death, divorce, injury, bullying, the loss of a job or perhaps a relocation of the family. Caring for a child at these times and using the crisis as an instrument of growth requires tact and sensitivity. Often the young person can be on an emotional roller-coaster and it takes an astute mentor to be a guide. Nonetheless, a crisis can spur growth if adults are able to discern the right moment and manner to engage the child and teach them about life. In our own family's experimentation with organised PROPs, we have found that they coincidentally and uncannily have taken place during times of unexpected crisis. We have been thankful during these times of unsolicited pain that the PROP enabled us to try to make some sense of what was happening, and, without exception, we have observed our boys maturing in the process.

It is important, however, not merely to rely on life's surprises to help the child mature. There is also need for organised PROPs; moments of adventure and ritual, thoughtfully and lovingly crafted with the aim of helping the boy become a man. The fact that a planned rite of passage is in the family calendar not only affirms the boy's importance but can also help diffuse inevitable moments of confrontation between parent and child. When things get hot and hurried in the day-to-day exchanges, the knowledge that a PROP is coming allows the adults to take a mental note of an issue and put it on the back burner until a time when a calm and constructive conversation can take place.

A few guidelines for building belief during a PROP

When planning the belief building element of a PROP, you may find the following guidelines helpful:

● *Men and women should be involved*
The boy should receive both male and female perspectives to enable him to develop a well-rounded view of life and the knowledge of the tools needed to navigate the next phase. The PROP could begin with a time of listening and learning from older guides and mentors. Mother and son time before and after the event is as important as father and son time.

● *Stories are effective*
Stories and testimonies are excellent means of conveying beliefs and values. The emphasis should be on shaping the boy's character and affirming his identity and heritage. He needs to know that the lessons learned will form the foundation on which he can build his own life.

● *Make use of multi-sensory learning*
Use natural resources to teach the lessons of life. For example, when talking about the vastness of God, point the boy to the sky and study the stars. It may not have been the first time he has done this, but in the context of a PROP, a memorable impression can spark a life changing decision. Be aware, though, that he may come up with more questions than you have answers. This is good, and you should let him work out some of the grand questions on his own.

● *Enjoy the bond*
Enjoy the stronger bond that will grow, for a PROP strengthens the connection between parent and child. The boy is likely to gain a fresh respect for you and develop a greater appreciation for what you have to teach him. He will lap up your 'war stories',[42] so use the PROP wisely. Do not overload, and ensure that you prepare thoughtfully what you teach, ensuring that the insights blend the practical with theory.

Summary

PROPs provide an ideal opportunity to ignite and/or strengthen a boy's belief system.

 **Key Points**

- While teaching inevitably takes place in everyday life, a PROP provides an opportunity to focus on what is coming up, and the waters the young person needs to navigate safely in the next stretch of life
- A PROP reminds the young person of the strength that is derived from their heritage and community values.

Tips

- Ensure that what you teach the boy is simple, practical and makes sense. The best way to make sure they have understood and embraced what you have said is to have them discuss examples with you in which the values and advice you have given them would be relevant.
- The book of Proverbs is an excellent resource to help the boy prepare for his PROP. I read it first when I was thirteen and my fourteen-year-old is reading it now. There is a lot of material relevant to boys in it! A month before a PROP the boy could begin reading a chapter a day. There are just enough chapters to complete within a month. The reading of Proverbs in the days and weeks leading up to the PROP can fuel the sense of anticipation of the adventure and inform his reflections; before, during and after the event.

3

Ceremony

In the Gospel of Luke, there is a remarkable story of a night that Jesus and three of his closest friends spent on a high place known as the Mount of Transfiguration. Imagine the shock and thrill experienced by the three friends when they awoke in time to catch the tail end of an extraordinary spiritual happening: the appearances of deceased prophets amidst a glorious swirling haze. Peter, perhaps wanting to contain, commemorate or even continue the experience, suggested building something. The story reveals not only the importance of spiritual retreat but also the unexpected fun and surprise that often comes with it. It also reminds us that we do not live in retreat. Rather, we are to return and live in the daily momentum and fray of life. Encounters with God should propel us off the mountain, reinvigorated, to engage life with clarity and renewed passion. In other words, a spiritual retreat is only purposeful if it prepares us for practical advance.

A PROP is not complete until the young person has returned and been welcomed back by the community. Such a reception marks the finale, much like the way a marathon runner enters the stadium after a long and arduous race, with cheering crowds, and crosses the finish line. If a rite of passage ends short of the finish line, and there are no crowds of cheering friends and family, the boy's passage will be incomplete. The closing ceremony is an essential conclusion to a puberty rite of passage. The communal act of welcoming the boy into manhood should have three elements: symbolism that the passage is complete, recognition of new responsibilities and privileges and a party that welcomes the boy into a new period of life.

> ### Symbolism
>
> 'A symbol is more the expression of something mysterious whose presence or existence... is simultaneously "internal" but distant. Through it our inner, unconscious or spiritual experience is united with our outer, sensory experience.'[43]
> John Baldock, *The Elements of Christian Symbolism*

Nelson Mandela, along with several of his peers, had a collective puberty rite of passage at the age of fifteen, which lasted several weeks. Near its conclusion, he was required to burn his blanket. The blanket was his companion during his six-week course, and came to represent his childhood. Its destruction gave a physical sign to the boy Mandela that his boyhood was ending and manhood was beginning. The burning of the blanket signified that no longer would he live in a protected environment of childhood with everything provided; from now on, he would take a greater responsibility for himself. It was an important putting away of childhood. The psychology of this is similar to the need, when someone has died, for the bereaved to view the coffin and the remains in order to accept the death. This visual aid helps them accept the loss and embrace the future. Likewise, the power of the symbolic gesture ensures an ongoing realisation that life is now different. Some rites of passage use a cord which is cut during the ceremony, indicating that the boy is freed from parental control and is now independent. Others use fire as a symbol. A short while ago, I was speaking at a conference in the UK on this subject. One of the men present told me about a church in Louisiana he had attended where the men and boys of the church would go on an adventure weekend as a rite of passage. The weekend concluded with a fire ceremony in which all the men would hold torches forming a corridor of fire. Each boy would pass through the corridor, then take his place in the line of men holding his own torch, symbolising his joining the community of men.

My friend, David McKenzie, has three sons and when each turned eighteen, he presented them with a key to the house granting them freedom to come and go as they pleased; expecting them, of course, to do so in courtesy to the others in the household. The key represented their independence and arrival as an adult. However, there was something more to the key ritual. There was a second part of the ceremony, which the sons were not aware. A few days after the eighteenth birthday party, David would take his son out for the evening. When they arrived home and walked up the path to the house, David would not use his key to open the door. Instead, he would wait until the son used his key. With each of his sons, the boy would wait for his dad, and look somewhat puzzled that his dad did not take out his key and unlock the door, as he had always done so before. Eventually, David would deliver the following speech:

Son, you are a man now, you have the key. You open it. Life is going to be full of doors and it is up to you whether you take out your key to open the door and walk through it. I will not be there for you from now on, it is up to you to open the door. You will come to many doors in your life and when you do, you will have a decision to make. Do you unlock and it and walk through, or do you stand in front of a closed door? The choice is yours. What will you do with the key and the door? When you have the key and you do not open the door, you have a problem.

> 'In symbolic action we take the known and lift it to the unknown so that it is returned to us as the mystery of the transcendent... The very narrative of faith which we seek to know and to live is symbolically expressed in space. We take the ordinary aspects of life – stone, wood, windows, tables and chairs – and form them into voices of Christian mystery... Communication in this model comes through an immersed participation in the event.'[44]
>
> Robert Webber, author of *Ancient – Future Faith*

When my older son Ryan climbed Mount Fuji as his rite of passage into adolescence, he purchased a walking stick, as do most pilgrims. Pilgrims climb the mountain – which they consider to be holy – reverently, using the stick as not only a tool but also a spiritual instrument. Tied on to the stick is a bell. Most of the way up we could hear the clanging of bells from the hundreds of pilgrims ascending the famous peak. Those coming down, however, walked in silence, still with the stick but no bell. Near the summit, there is a shrine where the pilgrims discard their bells before continuing their ascent in silence. I am not sure of all the reasons for the practice, but Ryan and I felt it right to redeem it for his rite of passage and invest it with Christian meaning. Ryan threw his bell onto the heap of bells as a symbol of his leaving pre-adolescent childhood. We then prayed, thanking God for Ryan's childhood, and asking for God's help for his adolescent years. Ryan kept the stick as a record of his climb and passage into adolescence. For many months after Ryan would scold me for referring to him as a child. His response always was 'I am an adolescent now!'

Recognition of new responsibilities and privileges

During the ceremony, recognition needs to be made of the boy's new privileges and duties. The awarding of new rights and responsibilities helps aids the mental and emotional acceptance of his maturity. Nelson Mandela, after his rite of passage, had the right to engage with the elders of the village. However, along with this privilege, he had the responsibility to engage thoughtfully with other men. He probably would not make much of an impression if he was to speak nonsense or engage the elders in frivolous chatter. Our culture is different but we can still apply the principle of the ceremonial bestowal of their rights and responsibilities. Increasing the boy's allowance, the acquiring of a driver's licence, allowing a later curfew, etc, are activities involving an increase in responsibility, where a matured standard of behaviour is expected. The increased responsibility should not just be in the realm of chores around the house, but also in a higher standard of social protocols: how to speak to people, sharing, serving and putting others first. The granting of privilege and responsibility helps the boy define the future he is stepping into as different from the past.

It helps him in practical terms to see the line he has crossed, and that he is waking from the dreamy state of boyhood to the very real and exciting world of manhood.

The presentation of the key by David McKenzie to each of his three sons was in part an implicit recognition of their new privileges and responsibilities. Practically, the boys already had a key but this new key symbolised adult freedom and responsibility. No longer did the son need to inform his parents where he was going and when he would return. As an adult member of the household, he was free to come and go as he pleased, but also he had a responsibility to be courteous and sensitive to those around him, respecting the others with whom he lived. A driver's licence, the coming of age allowing alcohol consumption, an increased allowance, more duties and responsibility for investments can further indicate to the community that a boy is becoming an adult.

A welcome party

> 'The best way to make your dreams come true is to wake up!'
>
> Paul Valery, poet and writer[45]

The ending of a PROP provides a great opportunity for a party, when the household and community celebrate the changes in the boy. It is vital that the teenager sees their growing up is a good thing for him and his family. The emphasis in the festivities should not be on a leaving but rather a welcoming. He is still part of the family and the church but he is now in a different role.

The party reinforces the fact that he is a part of something larger, and that everyone is relishing his mature participation in community affairs. This aspect of feeling good about himself is liberating for the young man. Men and women, fathers and mothers should have equal roles and profiles in the ceremony and the party. It is important to everyone concerned that the boy is becoming an adult. However, at some point the father or a father figure should step forward and welcome the boy into the fraternity of men. This gesture from a respected older man can seal in the young man's soul an inner confidence that he is trusted and is a man.

Guidelines for ceremonies

In the final chapter of this book, we will explore what the church can do to help in the ceremonial aspect of a PROP. Churches have many traditions, symbols and liturgies that can be drawn upon to bring closure to a boy's rite of passage and send him off as a man to make a difference in the world. But whether in or outside the church, you may want to adhere to the following principles when organising a ceremony.

- Avoid the cringe factor. Think carefully through what symbols are used and their meaning.
- Do not overload with too many symbols. The memory of one or two symbolic acts can last a life time.
- Men need to be present and to be the lead participants. Only men can welcome boys into the fraternity of men.
- Involve siblings, particularly older brothers who have grown up and left home.

Summary

A PROP needs an ending to bring to a close all that the boy has experienced. The church and family can gather around him to celebrate and commemorate his passage. The ceremony should contain a bestowal of new rights and responsibilities.

 Key Points

- The return should include symbolism, a party and commissioning
- The boy has become a man, and the return does not symbolise a leaving of his clan but the acceptance of a new role within it.

Tips

The participants for the party should include all those who have an interest or role in teaching and guiding the child. For example, extended family, pastors, teachers, coaches, close friends of the family as well as peers. At the celebration, choose a meaningful symbol that will help the boy remember the PROP and the day he crossed over into manhood.

Part Three

Growing boys

1

What boys need to know

Life is a rite of passage. From the earliest development in the womb, leading to the journey through the birth canal, the lifelong principle of entering and leaving is established. The transitions of life all originate in the leaving of one phase to enter another. Each phase is a preparation for the next passage. Whether your son is a toddler, about to begin school, or having to move location with you, the opportunity presents itself to mark the occasion. This will help him both accept the change and rise to new challenges. While the main PROP should come in the late teen years, there could be a series of mini-PROPs as the child grows up. From the toddler years onwards, boys will benefit from mini-adventures mixed with family ceremonies and teaching times. The need for mini-PROPs only increases when the boy enters his adolescent years.

Adolescence is not only long, it is also dangerous. Harville Hendrix and Helen Hunt, co-authors of *Giving the Love that Heals*, suggest that adolescence has three distinct periods:

Stage one: the onslaught of puberty

Stage two: mid-adolescence marked by a 'pre-occupation with the opposite sex that throws the established order out of balance'

Stage three: late adolescence, a 'period of preparation when the young person becomes concerned with the tangible tasks of dealing with his future.'[46]

To their list of three, I would add a fourth: post-adolescence, which marks the lifelong process of growing up, the inevitable passage through mid-life and the eventual emergence as an elder in the community. Through all of these phases, the boy is learning the facts of life about his gender, his relationships, his spirituality and his property. We will take a brief look at mini-PROPs for the adolescent before we look at some possible ideas for the main PROP that will initiate the boy into manhood. Whatever period a boy may be in, he is on a constant journey of discovering about the basics of life. For each period of life, the boy needs to learn more about the fundamentals. Before we take a closer look at mini-PROPs for the adolescent and the main PROP, I want to outline general issues that a boy needs to learn about through all the phases of growing up.

When our boys stepped from the path of childhood into the adventure Big Impossible, we told them that life would speed up for them as adolescents. Changes were coming and they needed new intellectual and emotional tools to navigate the adolescent years. We explained that physiological changes would take place naturally but that with those changes, they would gain greater power in making choices. These changes and choices would affect their bodies, minds and relationships, their spirituality and their money. It was an outline we found useful, for it covered the basics of a boy's development right through all their leaving and entering stages. Never are the boy and his family more acutely aware of these changes than in the teenage years.

His body

Bodily changes in a boy arouse great curiosity, and can create a sense of being different, if not explained as normal. His body is leaving its childish shape in order to become an adult. He may need to hear a parent or a mentor say that all is normal and that the pace of change is different for each person. This is important, as boys will find an opportunity to compare! The emergence of pubic hair, a change in voice, intensifying sexual drive, wet dreams etc, can cause alarm if not expected. He needs to hear from you that his body will change, how it will change, and that it may not change at the same speed as that of others in his peer group. He must feel normal. If the boy grows too fast, he may appear clumsy to others or perhaps use his powerful body unwisely. Equally, he may develop more slowly, resulting in him overcompensating, perhaps by using words to fight his battles. If the boy knows that his mind, body and soul may not develop at the same pace, he will be more at peace within himself and with others. There are many books, such as James Dobson's *Bringing up Boys* and Steve Biddulph's *Raising Boys* that can help provide more information. To know more about the hormonal fluctuations and how they affect bodily development and behaviour can help a parent be more patient with their sons.

When I learned about the facts of life

My dad did not find it easy informing me about sex. His father had died when my dad was three. This left him bereft of a role model. No one had passed onto him the ancient insights of the timeless activity of sex. I am not sure whether it was his shyness on the subject or my simply being 'thick' that slowed the process down. I often joke that when my dad first told me about the birds and bees, I was stung two days later by a bee and was terrified I had become pregnant. I was confused even more when he tried to use arithmetic: $1 + 1 = 3$. Quite simply, it did not add up. It was finally at the age twelve in 1967 that I learned the truth.

My father, an itinerant evangelist, was conducting a mission at a church. Feeling the church premises needed livening up a bit, particularly for the children's meetings, I had wondered what I could do to help. The answer to my prayer came in the form of a sock full of flesh coloured sausage shaped balloons. What they lacked in colour they made up for in elasticity and size. I nearly hyperventilated blowing the balloons up and I vaguely recall making happy faces and writing Scripture verses on some of them before distributing them throughout the church and the car park. Folks began to gather as I stood at the door, proud of my decorative skills. My father eventually arrived with the minister by his side. I was there to greet them and receive their grateful thanks for my creative endeavour. I had strategically placed myself by the pulpit with a large silly grin on my face. My father and the minister were a stride or two into the hall when they were halted by the sight of the balloons.

Dad was dumbfounded as he scanned the hall taking in the grand scale of my artwork. Eventually his eyes focused on the large inflated memory verse protruding from the pulpit and me standing beside with a beaming smile. The silence broke with his booming question: 'Where did you get those?'

I answered with naïve pride for all to hear: 'Out of your sock, dad!' He quickly ushered me out of the hall, sat me down and proceeded to tell me, in unambiguous terms, what I needed to know about sex. I was shocked to hear the true purpose of those balloons.

His mind

Education is important in today's world. Modern society emphasises not only the need for a good education when you are young but also the need for lifelong learning. One of my mentors, David McKenzie, who leads HOPE International Development Agency, has also become a mentor to my sons. On a recent trip to Canada, Ryan had to return to Japan ahead of me for the beginning of a new school term. He had been travelling with me as I spoke at a series of events organised by HOPE. On the eve of his departure, when Ryan was saying that he wanted to stay longer, David, with a tease in his voice, said to Ryan, 'Tell your dad he should not let your schooling stand in the way of your education.' David was giving light-hearted affirmation to Ryan for taking a week out of school to come with me to Canada.

We need to foster enthusiasm for formal education, but also to develop a hunger to learn experientially too. My son had the privilege of a learning experience that involved travel, but experiential learning need not only involve making a trip. Building awareness through the reading of newspapers, wise use of the internet, joining clubs and associations can all help expand a boy's horizons. However, do not rule travel out because of finances. There are many low cost opportunities and innovative ways to fund international travel these days. My wife and I live on missionary incomes, but we chose long ago to make travel for our children a priority. We want them to become globally aware and not parochial in their vision of life.

His relationships

As boys grow older, their relationships are in a constant state of re-definition. Social skills need constant development and refinement. Human beings, all made in God's image, deserve to be treated with dignity and respect and the basic teaching of Christianity is to love our neighbours as ourselves. We encourage our children to seek peace rather than conflict. While teaching our boys that they are growing into independent adults, they need to have the security of knowing that they will always be part of an interdependent community. Adolescents need the accrued wisdom of their families and the guiding fraternity of mature friends. Although it sounds contradictory, it is critical that during adolescence a child should feel connected. He must learn to value the reservoir of people, history and shared values that have helped form him. This is not at the exclusion of peers – quite the opposite: the adolescent needs to feel part of their own generation – but it need not be at the expense of his family. The social sinew that keeps them connected across the generations needs to be strong, for the boy will draw strength from the knowledge that he belongs.

Phil Jackson, the basketball coach who led Michael Jordan and Chicago Bulls to the NBA Championships for most of the nineties, wrote in his book, *Sacred Hoops*: 'Good teams become great ones when the members trust each other enough to surrender the "me" for the "we."'[47] The aim of the PROP is not for the boy to become distant from the clan, family and household that brought him up, but rather for him to reconnect with it as a functioning adult participant. The success of a boy entering adulthood depends largely on the way he leaves adolescence. The knowledge gained in the previous stage will be foundational in the next.

His spirituality

It is a joy to talk to a child about God in an earthy manner, outside of the four walls of a church building. A PROP, at whatever stage of transition, provides an excellent opportunity. The child needs to know that God is not only present in times of collective worship but is a companion in all of life. The role of prayer needs to be explained practically and inspirationally, and not taught as a 'must do' but as a privilege that can be enjoyed in everyday life.

Life is multi-faceted, but we never get beyond learning the basics. We hope that our boys will grow up with a deep sense of curiosity for all aspects of life.

His money

We live in a material world and our young people are materially minded. We are raising young consumers, like it or not, and they need to be taught the place that money has in life and how to subjugate its power. Children learn early the thrill of buying: therefore, we must teach them early practical and biblical principles of financial management. I have found Richard Foster's writings on money in his book *Money, Sex and Power* useful in teaching my own boys about money matters.[48] Foster outlines four biblical financial management principles:

- *Stewardship*: everything we have belongs to God
- *Taxes*: we have a responsibility to society and our families, therefore we must pay our taxes and plan for the long-term financial health of our household
- *Investment*: it is good to grow our money in a responsible fashion as Christ affirmed in his parables
- *Giving*: God wants us to give our money to the poor

With each son, we outlined Foster's teaching on money and stressed that money has great power. We explained that either you make it surrender to you or you come under its spell – and if that happens, you jeopardise your soul. Practically, we also gave them a lump sum of cash and increased their allowances after each mini-PROP. It is important that this should happen as a consequence of a rite of passage.

Summary

At all stages of their growing up, boys need to learn relevant lessons about their sexuality, their minds, their relationships, their spirituality and their possessions.

Key Points

- The main PROP comes in the late teen years when the boy is about to assume manly responsibilities, but mini-PROPs can help ease the boy through all periods of change
- Relevant and practical information needs to be given to the boy to help him understand and anticipate changes that are taking and will take place.

2

Mini-PROPs for the budding adolescent

> 'Adolescence is the time for risk for boys, and that risk taking is also a yearning for initiation.'
>
> Robert Bly[49]

When Ryan and Mac each turned ten, we planned a mini-PROP to mark their entry into adolescence. It was an adventure with a theme designed to prepare them for the next two–three years of their lives. Together as a family, we positively anticipated their first PROP experience and, as parents, we prayed that it would both buoy and propel them through the early adolescent years. We felt that perseverance should be the theme. As we have seen, Ryan chose to climb a mountain while Mac opted for a swimming challenge. Each challenge required determination to 'stick with it'. We enjoyed observing them in the hard grind of perseverance and as they earned the warm glow of achieving the goal. They seemed happy that we remained close by, acting not only as cheerleaders but as coaches too, when necessary!

The achievement was theirs but in a sense ours too, for we had put much of ourselves into it, in terms of planning and participation.

Kande and I noticed that, psychologically, each of our boys emerged from the experience with a confidence and interest in the changes that were coming. They seemed to acquire a sense of place and an appreciation for their inner compass that would help them find their way. They seemed to understand that the journey would not be easy but that they would not need to face it alone. Each mini-PROP was tailored to the boy and his interests at the time. Nevertheless, both boys' events involved others. Mac had the added blessing of his extended family, while Ryan climbed Mount Fuji not only with me, but also in the company of a group of men. With each son's entry into adolescence, we tried to tailor the experience to their interests with the belief that if they wanted to do it, they would be much more likely to persevere. Your children will have different ideas and needs. You may want to focus on themes other than perseverance. That is fine. Whatever the theme, make sure it is clear and relevant to the activity that has been planned.

Mac's mini-PROP

Ryan, my older son asked to climb Mount Fuji for his rite of passage, while Mackenzie decided on a different challenge when he turned ten nearly three years later. He chose to set a personal record by swimming two thousand metres. His adventure coincided with a trip I had to make to Canada for my nephew's wedding, which meant his grandparents could be involved. Mac and I spent a week together travelling, setting aside one full day for the rite of passage. The day started with a hearty breakfast at a local restaurant, during which Mac's two grandfathers shared stories of their lives and lessons they had learned. After breakfast, we went to the pool. With the keen interest of the lifeguards and under the caring watch of his extended family, Mac donned his goggles and began his challenge. It took him just under two hours, and he climbed out of the pool to the applause of family and new friends, glowing with his achievement.

The day was not over as the swimming challenge was followed with a session of indoor rock climbing in order for Mac to experience the thrill (and fear) of vertical ascent. For two hours, he learned the importance of skills and stamina and overcame a mild but very real fear of heights. The grandparents came to watch and then joined us along with aunts, uncles and cousins at a restaurant to celebrate Mac's achievements and his becoming an adolescent. Between the climbing and the meal, Mac and I spent two hours alone talking about his life and the changes that he would be experiencing as a young adolescent. At the meal, prayers and blessings were pronounced on Mac.

Mac had chosen swimming because he said he did not like climbing mountains. He said that he tired too quickly. Six weeks after our return to Japan, while on holiday in the mountains, Mac surprised me when he said he wanted to climb Mount Fuji. Ryan was eager to climb it again, so the three of us set out together, with my wife taunting me that I still had some catching up to match her record of six climbs. It was a joy to see my two sons scurry up the mountain together.

Even more, I appreciated their patience with me as I hobbled back down with my knees caving in, slowing my descent considerably.

Pre-adolescence PROPs – ideas

I have come across many good ideas for mini-PROPs for entry into adolescence:

- Some parents take their pre-teens on a mission trip
- Father and son weekends. Here in Japan, members of the foreign Christian community in Tokyo plan 'stress camps'. These retreats are for fathers and sons and usually involve several days of hacking and hiking through mountainous jungle
- Mother and son night out on the town
- Charity walks. I went on my first charity walk at the age of twelve, and the experience influenced the course my life.

My friend, Jonny Baker, the former London Director of Youth For Christ and now the National Youth Co-ordinator for the Church Missionary Society and father of two sons, Joel and Harry, marked their entry into adolescence in a particularly exciting and but meaningful way. The three of them have given me permission to include their experience in this book. Jonny believes in the power of ritual. He decided that when each of the boys turned ten, they needed an experience that would allow them to say goodbye to the first ten years of their lives and to welcome the next ten years.

In pondering what kind of ritual to use, Jonny did not want anything too 'heavy or intense'. He decided to take them into London for the day, which began with a father and son chat in a sports café. They talked about their first ten years and each 'reflected that in ten years time he would be a man.' They then went on to the Pepsi Max Drop in London. It is a free fall ride where you are strapped in and then slowly taken up. Jonny describes 'an agonising pause at the top and then you suddenly drop hundreds of feet to the ground.' Jonny had told each boy that when they got to the top, they should 'shout "Goodbye first ten years" and free fall into the next ten.' It was 'good fun' and they each got a photo taken as they were falling. Harry, the younger son, had written on a piece of paper things he remembered from the first ten years and as they fell he threw it into the air which 'amazingly' was captured in the photo as it floated in the air.

What ideas come to your mind? I have listed below some possibilities to spark your brainstorming. Remember, though, it is important to identify a theme and purpose for your child's mini-PROP. Be clear as to what they will learn, for the knowledge gained will give them the tools they need to build their characters. Use the imaginative genius that lies within your family and your church to create a relevant mini-PROP for a child who is about to enter the adolescent years.

Summary

Adolescence begins early and therefore you should too in preparing your children for its arrival.

Key Points

- Children should not be surprised by the changes that will come in their minds and bodies. Tell them clearly what to expect and when it may happen
- The mini-PROP marking their passage into adolescence need not be long or elaborate, but does need to be meaningful
- Invite the boy to offer ideas
- Early adolescents will benefit from learning the value of perseverance.

Tips

Ensure the child is aware of the mini-PROP well ahead of time. The anticipation will make the experience a richer one but also it will give plenty of time for the young person to absorb the meaning of the mini-PROP and understand that it is for his benefit. Plan now to have a conversation with your son, and introduce the prospect of a mini-PROP to him.

Ideas

- A navigation theme: take the boy on an orienteering challenge or something similar.
- Abseiling.
- Triathalon: choose three activities that are appropriate to the age and interests of the boy. They do not need to be all sports or a physical challenge. For example, if the child is interested in science, then include an ambitious science experiment, or if he likes art, then the PROP could involve a project in making something.

- Take the child on a history tour of family sites: places of birth, schools, old neighbourhoods etc. and talk about the past and the values of your family.

3

Helping in the battle at midway (ages 14-16)

> 'We need our boys to turn into young men who will care about others and be part of the solutions of the twenty-first century.'
>
> Steve Biddulph[50]

Mini-PROPs can also be helpful through the years of mid-adolescence which can be a tortuous time for adolescent and parent alike. Testosterone levels for the boy are 800 per cent higher than they were three to four years previously and the body seems to be growing in disproportionate measure to maturity. At one moment, you have an adult in the house and at the next moment a toddler. Added to the hormonal adjustments taking place are the pressure of exams in school and a greatly increasing social network. The boy is increasingly self-conscious as he tries to cope with the changes he is going through in order to become a man, even though he may not show it. He is caught somewhere between the child he sees reflected in the rear-view mirror and the manhood to which he eagerly aspires. It seems at times that the child wants the best of both worlds: the relative irresponsibility of childhood and the autonomous life of a grown-up.

It is critical at this time that the teenager understands that what is taking place in his mind, body and spirit is normal. Often, the adolescent can display moments of arrogant self-appreciation and then show a thinly veiled abhorrence for the ugliness of his body, with some parts such as feet changing at a greater pace than the rest. During this period, a father or another respected male figure has a timely opportunity to speak affirmation into the boy's life, reassuring him that what he is experiencing is nothing new; every man alive has walked the same road, passing from the old to the new. A caring adult can provide moments when the teenager can see beyond himself and begin developing the people skills necessary for healthy relationships later in his life.

Questions of self-doubt and deep considerations will taint glowing visions of the future. This is normal and healthy. Adults must be aware that it is at this age when the philosophical basis of life is often forged.

A life decision

When I was twelve, in the back seat of my parents' car listening to music they had banned, I made a decision that nearly ruined my life. I decided to 'ditch God' and his influence and live my life the way I wanted to. I thought the decision would liberate me from the constraints of my parents' expectations. The year was 1968, and as a budding teenager and 'flower child', the perceived gap between my parents and my peers was widening by the day. Everything about my life as a minister's son seemed peculiar and I resented being different. I wanted to be the same as others; to grow long hair, smoke pot and 'love everybody right now.' For the next four years, I lived with the consequences of that decision. I had expected that my decision would bring my life into the age of glorious Technicolor but it stayed in black and white and, even worse, the picture became fuzzy and dark. I struggled with fear, self-doubt and nihilism for most of my middle teenage years. What acted as a counter to my debilitating thought-life was a mini-PROP of sorts. It was my first experience of raising money for the poor by participating in the thirty-five mile sponsored walk mentioned earlier. My parents supported me in this and as my house was five miles from the finishing line, they told me to plan to pop in when I was on the final stretch, which I did. Well, rather than popping in I crawled. I managed to get to the front door, but the stairs were a challenge and I only managed them going on all fours. I was exhausted. My mother immediately set about cooking me a meal while my father washed my feet. Thirty minutes later, I shot out the door with a full stomach and fresh socks to finish the walk, and called my parents an hour and a bit later, victoriously telling them I had crossed the finishing line. While it took a few years to sort out its implications for me in terms of life's vocation and values, it was a defining moment in my understanding of self. The adventure of helping others served to counterbalance my desire to distance myself from my parents' faith. I was discovering that Christian virtue is best – and perhaps only – displayed in the compassionate service of others.

Realising that egocentric behaviour is tempered by exposure to the needs of others, my wife and I decided that Ryan's second mini-PROP should focus on people. Once he turned thirteen, we wanted him to come face to face with world poverty and be challenged to make a difference.

Ryan's mid-adolescence mini-PROP

An opportunity arose for Ryan to accompany me on a visit to the Lumads in Mindanao, a war-torn island in the southern Philippines where HOPE International Development Agency, for whom I work, have a number of sustainable agriculture projects. We would spend a week touring the projects with a film crew from Canada. However, Ryan's PROP was to be more than a week in the Philippines. It started weeks before. As part of the service component of his PROP, Ryan set out to raise money for the projects among the Lumads. Not to be outdone by his brother, Ryan decided to swim four thousand metres in a sponsored swim. One week before Christmas and his thirteenth birthday, he went to a pool and swam four thousand metres. He raised over five hundred pounds.

The Lumads are indigenous people displaced from their mountain forest habitat in Mindanao to the valleys and forced to become farmers. Only two out of five children make it to the age of eight. The Lumads are not only in the vice of drought, water-born diseases, and the dark side of globalisation: they are also living in a war zone. Two months after his swim, Ryan and I went to Mindanao for one week in order to observe the effect of the 'learning farms' on the Lumad communities. His teachers were supportive and he went with their blessing. Ryan took the lead on things spiritual and asked to wear a cross. Together we prayed prayers from the Celtic Night Prayer Book each evening. We travelled in a group and avoiding areas where there was risk of kidnapping. Ryan turned out to be quite useful to the film crew. When we visited our first learning farm in a community called Nabawang, he served as 'Pied Piper', leading all the children from the locations where the film crew were conducting interviews. His day with the boisterous children stands out as the highlight of the trip. After several days of bone-jarring travel through mountainous territory, Ryan and I spent our final afternoon snorkelling and enjoying the wonders of the sea. It gave us an opportunity to talk about his experience.

It will take years and many more visits for Ryan to make up his own mind as to what his responsibility is as a member of a comparatively wealthy society to those who are poor. However, I am confident that the sights and sounds of his Mindanao adventure will stick with him and be a frame of reference, which will be of use to him in making important decisions in the future.

After returning from the Philippines, Ryan had a further opportunity to reflect on and work through the sights, sounds and smells of his Mindanao experience. During the Easter holidays, he accompanied me to Canada and participated in a series of fund-raising dinners organised by HOPE in aid of the Lumads. He seemed to enjoy his role as an advocate for the poor as he read the words of poems that I had written, inspired by our visit.

This year, Ryan is graduating from middle school and progressing on to high school within the international school he attends. We have realised as a family that there is a need and opportunity for another rite of passage, so this summer he will spend time with both his grandfathers, to be followed by a twenty-four hour solo camping trip. It will be a small version of a vision quest, for he will spend time   asking God for strength for the final four years of his pre-university education. You may find similar opportunities, in the early to mid teens, for 'adventures with purpose'.

Ryan's mini-PROP at the age of fourteen this summer is as much for my benefit as it is for his. Recently I have realised that I have a tendency to keep him young and it is difficult, from my emotional perspective, to keep pace with his growth into manhood. During his twenty-four hours alone, I also will be praying and asking for God's strength to recognise that Ryan is becoming a man.

Summary

Mid-adolescence is a time of self-absorption and it will serve the teenager well if their PROP is focused on people and the needs of others.

 Key Points

- The teenager will benefit from an 'out of culture experience'
- Ensure the integration of a spiritual element into the mini-PROP
- Don't let the mini-PROP end at the end of the mini-PROP: extend its shelf life by recording it on video, in a journal or through poetry
- Explain it to, and gain the support of, the child's teachers.

Tips

The mini-PROP at midway can easily be a joint parent and child experience. Unlike the final PROP in late teens, the young person needs to know that a parent or caring adult is close and they will benefit from seeing behaviour and reactions modelled for them. I was talking with a young man recently who coped remarkably well with a very nasty email message. He dealt with it maturely and said that because he had observed one of his teachers recently deal with a conflict situation philosophically and refuse to be riled, he had felt confident responding in the same way.

Ideas for mid-adolescent PROPs

I recommend a five to ten day experience for boys who have become teenagers. The project will require more preparation and greater budget than the first PROP that marked entry into adolescence. However, the process should involve the boy. Use them to spark and develop your own ideas:

● Triathlon: choose three activities/challenges that will suit and stretch the boy. Not all should be physical, for the challenge needs to be to the heart and mind as well. For example, you could blend a service project and a writing challenge with a long trek or bike ride.
● A week on a farm. Place the teenager on a working farm for a week either in the UK or abroad.
● A video diary of a journey. Plan a three to five day route requiring challenge and a responsible measure of risk through new territory. It could be trekking the Brecon Beacons, cycling in the south of France, walking the Great Wall of China, or traversing London by

foot. An adult companion should accompany the boy
but not interfere with decisions except for safety reasons. The adult companion could also have a camera
and take photos/videos of the boy on his journey.
After returning home, the boy could edit the video
and produce a short film.

- Take a trip to a large city (i.e. London, Glasgow, New
York) and join a team with an agency that works with
the homeless.
- Senseless: my mother suggested to me the idea of
including periods of time when the teenager is perhaps blindfolded or wears ear pads simulating what it
would be like to live without the use of one or more of
his senses. The discovery could trigger greater empathy for those who are physically challenged.

All of these ideas could involve a fund-raising element
and thereby easily remind the boy how service to others
can be integral in all he does.

4

The main event: prayer and purpose for the young adult (ages 18-20)

> 'One of the hallmarks ... of growing into manhood is the idea of defending and advancing a cause.'
> Roy McCloughry[51]

I have been involved in coaching basketball players for a number of years. I accepted the invitation to coach, despite feeling very inexperienced, because there was no one else able or willing to do so. I felt it would be a good way for me not only to interact with my two sons, who had developed an interest in basketball when we lived in the UK but also a helpful way to get to know the boys in the school. I have observed many boys over the last six years develop physically, mentally and socially. The school my boys attend in Japan is a multi-racial one with children from over twenty countries of Asia, the Americas, Europe and Africa.

It has been an interesting exercise in seeing how the pace of development is different for each boy. One thing is certain, though, there comes a day when the boy

leaves school and is faced with real world responsibilities. Some boys seem ready for it, while others look quite
fearful and stunned when the realisation hits them that
they have to leave home now and fend for themselves at
college or the work place. For most of the boys, the
leaving of school also means a physical move away from
their immediate families, and back to their home countries or a third country to attend university or college.
Some of the boys seem ready for it while others quite
evidently are not.

A series of mini-PROPs throughout adolescence can
help the boy to anticipate positively his eventual coming
of age. Once he is in his late teens or early twenties, it is
time for the all-important PROP that signifies and
celebrates that he is now a man. Often I look at boys I
know and can see that their parents have instilled in
them values and purpose. I watch how they interact
with their mum, dad or other adults and there is clear
evidence of maturity and the respect for self and others.
Other boys, I regret to say, appear to have parents who
have simply left them to drift into adolescence and I fear
for them and the unsuspecting world.

Our family is yet to experience a PROP that celebrates
the boy becoming a man. I suppose that is why I am
watching closely the development of boys older than my
own sons. One thing is for sure – we are committed to
providing them with a PROP experience that is significant and we are already saving up to do so. The
mini-PROPs that marked the entrance and midway
points of adolescence have helped our boys grow emotionally and spiritually and they have understood better
the road to adulthood rather than being confused.

There are moments of frustration and confusion for all
involved in the raising of any child but the final PROP
will mark the moment when the line is crossed and the

boy is welcomed into manhood. The three building blocks: adventure, belief and ceremony, when blended together, will create a memory for the young man and his community and be the catalyst for the inner transformation that the boy needs to know that he is now a man. The church should therefore soak the PROP in prayer and expect a significant spiritual experience. The PROP should have circumstances that are conducive to hearing the quiet whispers of God and experiencing the ferocity of passion and thrill of vision.

The timing of the PROP could incorporate the receiving of a driver's licence, graduation from school or college, or the young man entering the workplace. However, the PROP itself needs to be more than these inevitable developments in the life of the boy.

> 'I feel like I'm on a road, at a huge intersection with thousand of streets, yet I'm at a loss. There is no one to tell me the way, no "999" in the real world. You can't just call up and say, "Hey, I need a destination, I need a place to go." Even if someone did tell me where to go, I wouldn't listen. Sometimes I feel like I'm going nowhere.'
>
> An A level student

My gap year in Mexico

When I was twenty, my gap year in Mexico served as my PROP. For the first time I lived alone and had to fend for myself; domestically, emotionally and spiritually. I spent the year working at an orphanage, taking care of bees and flying as a second pilot to remote villages in the mountains, dropping aid. I drove back to Canada at the end of the year a different person. My family perceived me differently as well. I arrived home during the third week of December and I became the focus of the Christmas celebrations. The week I spent travelling three thousand miles in my small pick-up truck through the southern and western states of the USA gave me the solitude necessary to reflect on my experiences and to listen to God. I discovered that the year away was an important time of development in my private thoughts and spiritual life. I came back with a clearer idea of who I was and what I wanted to do with my life.

Solitude is an important element of the final PROP. Guides are to be nearby but not intrusive. I had older pilots and missionaries available, but for the most part, they only counselled me when I asked. Their friendship was a comfort to me and I appreciated their advice. Most of all, they modelled service to others. This is the final time for the young adult to consider again their inter-connectedness with others and the value of service. There is nothing like a sacrificial, body numbing, mind bending, and heart-breaking act of service to put the late adolescent's priorities and sense of self in order. It could be a two-week or two-month activity followed by a per-sonal retreat. Service is essential for the budding man to see himself and his world through the lens of the larger world. It will encourage him to embrace tenderness and empathy. He will always remember that part of becom-ing a man was the learning of service.

Doug Barnett, a veteran Christian leader told me that at the age of eighteen, he was obliged to enlist for two years in the Royal Navy.

The discipline, drill, physical demands and mental demands made upon me accelerated my progress from adolescence to manhood. Being taken from home and plunged into a mess deck life-style and then spending nearly two years on board ship really grew me. The experience of foreign lands and meeting different cultures, life-styles, food and customs broadened my outlook on life and appreciation of a world beyond my island home. I learned how privileged I was and how much I had to learn from others. I was a very young Christian at the time, just three months a believer when I joined up, and this aspect of my life was revolutionised. I owe my spiritual foundations to life in the Navy and the input of believers from many cultures into my life and thinking. The hardship and dangers of those two years were also character forming. I learned that nothing concentrates your mind like the four days and nights I spent in a force eleven hurricane.

Because of his experience in the Navy, Doug is a firm believer in a gap year of Christian service overseas. 'To get onto a work project or service orientated project in a different culture, area, nation' helps young people to 'confront themselves and their own vulnerability and discover their need for dependence upon God and others. They are faced with the harsh reality of life outside their own privileged western life-style. As a consequence they learn to be givers.'

Prayer

The boy is maturing. He has survived the traumas of mid-adolescence and he is about to cross the threshold into manhood. He has developed values and the mini-PROPs have helped prepare him for an adult role. If he has not already, the young man needs to develop spiritual disciplines: particularly he needs to develop finesse and confidence in prayer. There is a difference between saying prayers and praying. I am not criticising the use of a prayer book or pre-written liturgies: my point is that whether the prayers are extemporaneous or borrowed, to be truly a prayer it must be heartfelt.

Prayer need not be restricted to words. Some young men may find it more liberating to use action, body gesture, art and mood in intercession. The young man, on his final PROP, could be encouraged to explore different forms of praying. For example, if the boy is interested in music, at the end of a wilderness experience he could make a percussion instrument and pound his prayers. On the other hand, there could be a pile of stones provided, say perhaps of thirty fist size smooth rocks, and the boy asked to create a prayer mound and a praise mound, over a period of several hours. Each time he thinks of something that he is grateful for he could take a stone and place it on the praise mound. Similarly, he could identify concerns of a personal or global nature and then offer prayers for those issues, and for each place a stone on the prayer mound. At the end of the time, the two mounds will show him, hopefully, how many good things there are in life and how much he needs God's help. Alternatively, poetry could be written or pictures painted. These suggestions may suit the boy who is interested in art and creative expression, while others may simply need a prayer book, written for the occasion and used for the duration of the PROP.

Purpose

The desired outcome of his prayers and communion is the emergence of values that will shape his life and a sense of where he is going. Not necessarily a specific plan, but a sense of purpose nonetheless. He needs to acquire a dream, a vision of the future, an awareness of what his life is about and what it can be; in other words, a sense of destiny. I am amazed at how many young men I meet who are nice, appreciated by women for their tenderness, very much in touch with their intuition and emotions, but boring. They have no drive. When pressed, they talk about dreams but have little determination to turn fantasy into reality.

I organised a graduation celebration many years ago for a class of high school students. It was a church function and my job as the committee chair was to put together a team and a programme for the class dinner. I asked a young executive who was already making a name for himself to be the speaker. I will never forget his illustration. He had secretly placed a £5 note under one of the seats of the unsuspecting graduates before they arrived. The theme of his talk was not only to dream but also to act to make the dream a reality. At the end of his talk, he asked all the graduates to stand up and look under their chairs. The young man shouted joyfully when he discovered the £5 note. Once the boy and his covetous co-graduates had settled down, the speaker concluded by saying, 'My point is simple: if you want to acquire treasure in life, get off your bottom and do something about it.'

Our boys need to have a sense of purpose that will motivate them and shape their decisions. They also need a healthy dose of patience and holy pragmatism. They need to learn that plans change, but dreams remain. Yes, life is full of curves, bends and unexpected circumstances but life's surprises bring contour and texture to life.

One of my favourite theologians is Kosuke Koyama, a missionary from Japan who wrote a number of books. In one of them, named *Three Mile an Hour God*, he wrote,

'The womb is not a cube.'[52] Koyama explains that humans work with straight lines but God works with curves. Have you ever wondered why rivers meander rather than taking the most direct route? It is not human to live our lives in straight lines. To consider any deviance from the most efficient route to be a waste of time and therefore a failure is quite simply misguided and rigid rationalism. We should nurture children to relish in the unexpected and savour unexpected bends in the road. However, what gives them a point of reference is what they see on the horizon: it is the goal, the ideal, the vision. The time set aside for prayerful action, the seeking of a dream and destiny could take an hour or two, several days or even several months.

My mother once told me the story of Florence Chadwick who gained international fame in 1950 when she swam the English Channel in a record time for a woman. Later she attempted to swim from Catalina Island to Los Angeles. However, the day was exceptionally cold, the visibility was poor, and tensions were unusually high because a large killer whale was nearby. When Chadwick stepped into the cold Pacific, she was not the same confident, hope-filled competitor who had conquered the English Channel. Chadwick's mother and trainer rode in a rescue boat alongside her and offered her encouraging words and warm drinks. However, when fog made it difficult to navigate, Chadwick's spirit was broken; she gave up hope, and returned to the boat, defeated. When she learned she had been less than a quarter of a mile from the shore when she left the water, she cried. 'If only I could have seen the shoreline', she said, 'I could have made it.'

The lesson my mother taught me is an important one: visualise your destination and know where you are going.

A lesson for a church leader

It cannot be overstated how important the PROP is for the family and friends of the young man. For it is not just the boy who needs to accept his manhood, but also the family, particularly the mum and dad. John Partington, an experienced church leader and a magistrate in Exeter told me this story. 'A number of years ago, after an excellent Sunday morning meeting, my son, who was about eighteen and already working, went to McDonalds with a number of other youths. Not knowing where he had gone but realising he had taken my car keys with him, I became somewhat agitated (to put it mildly). When he eventually arrived back at the church with his mates, I began yelling. "Where have you been? Why didn't you tell me? You left me stranded!!" On giving me back the keys, Aaron went inside the church extremely upset and cried. My friend and fellow church leader wisely took me aside and reminded me that if anyone else of that age had taken my keys, by mistake, I would not have shouted and embarrassed them as I had done my own son. He was now a man in his own right and deserved the same respect I would have shown others. He was right. I realised I had a lesson to learn. Yes, I was his father but now I was also to be his "adult" friend and I needed to understand this new and natural progression in our relationship building. Aaron did not come home that night. He had stayed at a friend's house and when I found out the next day where he was, I arranged to meet him. I apologised profusely which he graciously accepted. There were plenty of hugs and tears. We had always had a good relationship and thankfully, that remains to this day. In fact, I can truthfully write he is one of my best friends.'

My friend, Dave Carlos, a Care for the Family team member, told me of something he did with his son when he turned eighteen. He wrote and designed a book about his son's life. It told of the joy he and his wife had felt at his birth and various stories of his growing up. Dave also wrote of what he felt about him now and their hopes for him in the future. It was not large: the eight pages were printed on special paper and only one copy was printed. Dave said, 'It meant a great deal to him and when, at a later date, someone asked if they could see what I had done, interestingly, he said, "No." It meant too much to him to have others seeing it.'

 Key Points

- Prayer should be emphasised in a PROP. But the young man should be encouraged to pray in a way that is heartfelt and appropriate for his circumstances and gifting
- If it hasn't happened already, a boy needs to acquire a sense of purpose, a call. A purpose is different to a plan. Plans change but values and call remain.

Summary

For the main PROP, in the late teens or early twenties, the budding adult needs to gain a clear sense of call and confidence that comes from an encounter with God.

Tips

- Invite the individual to articulate their dream and vision of the future. It may be that the young man does not have a clarity about specifics, but by this point in his life he will or should have through the PROP experience, a clear sense of values that will guide his life... serving his neighbour, caring for others. Alternatively, if he is bold and has a dream to become a politician, or a doctor, or a teacher, or a carpenter, or a house-husband, or a missionary, let him articulate it.
- Take a moment now with your son and affirm his becoming a man, and ask him to set aside some time with you in the next week or two to talk about what he would like to do to mark his coming of age.

Ideas for PROPs marking the final passage into adulthood

The PROP could last anywhere from one month to one year. Here are some ideas to provoke your own imagination.

- A gap year concluding with a welcome home party and ceremony of commissioning into adult life.
- Another triathlon: this should be bigger and better than before. It could include a service project in the

UK or abroad, or a major physical ordeal with a mental challenge.

- A journey, more ambitious than the last one. A photo journal or video diary could also be planned for this age. But this one should last for an extended period and the diary should not so much focus on 'him' but rather on what he discovers about people. For best results, the journey should have a theme.
- Leadership development. Send him on a management training course to hone his inter-personal skills.
- Plan and lead an expedition or short-term mission. This would focus on leadership development and involve the elements of fund-raising, promotion, logistical planning etc.
- If the young adult is an artist, he could put on a show or exhibition of his work and the work of others, with your support, to raise money for charity.
- Start a small business or investment portfolio. Commission him to put together a business plan, and offer him a small amount of money as an investment. Not all families or boys would be able or interested, but for the budding businessman, this could help bring a focus to some good ideas and give him a boost of confidence and motivation.

Part Four

What do we do now?

1

Extend the family

You will have heard the old African proverb 'It takes a village to raise a child.'[53] It's true. Mums and dads are essential, but the closer a child comes to adulthood, the more interaction they need with the extended family and a network of adult friends.

> 'What boys need most to conquer the Big Impossible – to survive the peer pressure, gender strait-jacketing, and the other tribulations of adolescence – is knowing that they have meaningful connections not only with their friends but also with parents and other family members.'[54]
>
> Dr Pollack, author of *Real Boys*

The notion that boys need to separate from their families is old and deserves to be filed away as an interesting but wrong theory. Yes, of course, boys need to become individuals or, as psychologists say, 'to individuate.' They need increased freedom, privacy and personal space, but this does not have to be at the expense of family relationships. Dr Pollack wrote: 'Our sons rarely wish to cut their ties, be on their own, or to separate from us. In fact, most of our boys desperately need their parents, the family, and the extended family to be there for them, stand firm yet show flexibility, and form a living wall of love that they can lean on and bounce off ... It's not separation but rather individuation they want.'[55] He goes on to say that it's a boy 'becoming a more mature self in the context of loving relationships – stretching the psychological umbilical cord rather than severing it – that healthy male adolescence is all about.'[56]

Our children need us! However, it often seems that they do not want us. I recently had a conversation with two fathers. One was the father of a daughter who had just turned thirteen. He was struggling to keep up with the fashions, music and issues that interested her. His despair was particularly acute because the CD he had bought her for her birthday present, which had been her favourite band a month before, was no longer on her list of preferred albums. He felt down because he was unable to keep up with her and concerned that his daughter changed her mind and tastes so quickly.

At this point, the other father spoke up and talked of his own relationship with his dad when he was a teen-ager. He told us of a conversation they had had the previous summer when he was visiting the family home with his young son. When he was a teenager, his father was always putting pressure on him for them to spend more time together. My friend said he had always resisted this. However, last summer his father surprised him and said that he was sorry for having put pressure on him and told him that he had been selfish and wrong to do so. Parents' love can be selfish at times. We have our own needs for love and acceptance and sometimes place expectations on our children to display their love for us in ways that satisfy us. However, I suggested to my friend that his father had no need to apologise. Research reveals that children need the active involvement of the adults who care for them. The challenge is to find appropriate ways to keep the sinew of a relationship strong, whilst allowing the boy to mature.

I am conscious that there are many families where, for a myriad of possible reasons, one of the parents is not at home. In some cases both parents are absent and grandparents, foster parents or friends of the family are bringing up the children. A boy needs a mother figure and father figure and for those adults in his life to be supplemented by a larger network of family. Where it is not possible for the biological parent to be involved in the life of a child, others need to step in and help to fill the gap.

In this chapter, I would like to highlight the role of mothers, fathers, grandparents and the rest of the extended family: aunts, uncles, cousins, etc.

Mothers

Boys need mothers. It is critical for a boy to grow up with an appreciation and respect for women. The boy who grows up with a woman providing maternal care should achieve this. There is a time, of course, when the relationship with the mother figure must change from one of dependence to interdependence, and this can be painful for the mother and in some cases traumatic for the boy too. However, the new relationship should be liberating for both as each finds a freedom in friendship.

Many cultures that practise puberty rites of passage place an emphasis on a son separating from his mother. In our culture, I believe this is unnecessary. A boy simply needs to redefine his relationship with his mother.

Mummy's boy

In Italy, the term *Mammismo*, which means Mummy's boy, is not a negative one, but rather celebrates the relationship between mother and son. According to David Pollack's research, '58 per cent of Italian "boys" between the ages of eighteen and thirty-four may live with their mothers.' Pollack quoted one young man who said: 'It's better to be loved at an older age than to be abandoned at a younger age... The kids who leave home at thirteen or fourteen in England are the ones missing something in terms of affection.'[57]

A PROP provides a wonderful opportunity for the redefining of the relationship to take place. The mother can celebrate her son becoming a man, and the boy can emerge into adulthood with a sense that his mother is pleased with and endorses his independence. She lets him go, knowing that she has imparted values and insights that will help him not only to survive, but also to thrive in an adult world. The relationship a boy has with his mother can provide the basis for a trusting, respectful relationship with all women.

I had a strained relationship with my mother. It was not her fault, but mine for choosing to reject the values she was teaching me. I decided to disregard her values at the age of twelve and, for several years, my mother became the object of my scorn and derision. It was a painful time for her. I was cocky, arrogant and dismissive of her. Yet she continued to love me, and I remained in reach of that love. Despite the cold shoulder I gave her, I was still aware of her love for me. I recall moments when I overheard her saying flattering things about me to others and I felt a surge of pride. Her words made me feel good about myself.

Later, in my teens, I decided to correct my ways. One night, at a Bible camp I decided to embrace the faith of my parents. It was quite a turn around. I spent an evening praying, trying to sort out my adolescent life with God. By the end of it, I felt liberated, cleansed and filled with a sense of goodness. Later that night, believing that God had forgiven me for my errant ways and nastiness towards my family, I sought my mother first in the family for forgiveness. As we hugged, I sobbed like a baby and told her how wrong I was to have treated her the way I did. My mother and I were reconciled that night, and although I still had a lot of growing up to do, and to this day we have lively disagreements, the basis of our relationship is mutual love and respect. Her love for me is unconditional. It is a mother's love.

Perhaps the hardest thing for a parent, particularly mothers, is letting go. I was talking with a woman the other day who is the mother of three adult children. I asked her, what was the toughest thing about being a parent? Without hesitation she answered, 'Learning to let go.' She paused, leaned forward and looking straight at me said: 'It doesn't get easier. I am still learning that lesson every day even though my kids have all left home.' While a mother's love will continue for a lifetime, a PROP helps the mother not so much to let go, but to welcome the boy into a new, adult friendship. The boy also benefits from knowing that his mother celebrates and affirms his becoming a man.

Father figures

'When I was a boy of fourteen, my father was so igno-
rant I could hardly stand to have the old man around.

> But when I got to be twenty-one, I was astonished at
> how much the old man had learned in seven years.
> Mark Twain, author of *The Adventures of Tom Sawyer*[58]

Mark Twain's quotation is famous. With wry humour, he captures the perspective many boys in their teens have on their fathers. My son Ryan, now fourteen, has told me more than once that he believes that I have forgotten what it is like to be his age. This is largely the boy creating a distance between himself and his father in order to become independent. The boy's natural compulsion to prove to himself that he can survive without his father's help, can result in a father feeling pushed away. As a result he may not engage with his son in the growing up process, as he should.

Almost all the men I interviewed felt that their fathers left them to drift through adolescence. This is wrong. Our sons need a father figure to be actively involved with them during their teen years. Steve Adkins is a chartered surveyor, church leader and former rugby player with the England squad. He loves sports and it was through sports that he connected with his father. His father went to every match and was Steve's private coach as he rose through the ranks of rugby. Steve never resented his father's presence nor thought it was odd that his father was around. Particularly when he was captain of the team, which he often was, his dad would give him valuable insights about leadership. Often, while driving home after practice, his dad would say to him something like, 'The way you dealt with that situation today was really good. Maybe next time you could try it this way.' Today, Steve and his father are the best of mates. Steve now has two sons of his own: one is seventeen and the other nineteen. They do not like rugby, but both are mad about golf. Steve has taken up golf himself and together they play in tournaments. The way his father interacted with him has provided Steve with a model of fatherhood that he has followed with his own sons.

Steve's story reminded me of a statement made by Robert Bly: 'Men are not male mothers.' Father figures are important to boys. While not all boys will be heavily into sports the way Steve and his sons are, boys do need a father figure with whom they can engage in boy things. I have a friend who is an artist. He is a reflective man and has never been into competitive sports. His son, now six years old, displays the same artistic traits. He is quiet, creative and thoughtful. Recently, the boy has surprised his parents by his need to wrestle with his father after supper each night. The mother could not understand where he got this need from. Another mother of two boys told me the same. Her primary school age sons have to wrestle with their father every night. Never do they try to wrestle with her. No sooner is their dad through the door than they are leaping on him and trying to pull him to the ground. Boys take something different from their father. They need a father figure with whom they can engage in rough and tumble. They do not want to wrestle with their mothers, but there seems to be a need to expend some of the testosterone that is surging through their changing bodies and to connect with a father figure.

My boys are no different. In the evenings, I will often be lured into the living room, where I am ambushed and we have a free-for-all on the floor. I did the same with my own father. He is not at all interested in sports but he would get down on all fours and engage with me at my level. I do not recall ever trying to wrestle with my mother but I always cherished the moments of physical contact with my father.

Boys want to become men, therefore it is men who need to welcome boys into the fraternity of men. Many men today have never been formally welcomed into manhood by men and consequently they have a lingering insecurity. Often they continue to be rebels, resisting authority as an attempt to declare their independence, or they become excessively submissive in order to win the approval of older males.

A father and son relationship is not easy. Sometimes there can be confrontation that seems to lead to an ongoing battle. Boys strive to reach their fathers' standards of strength and power and sometimes there is friction. The battle is played out in all kinds of ways: through physical sports but also in verbal and mental games. The boy will often challenge his father. If he is not doing it outwardly, he will be doing it inwardly. That is why adolescence can be stressful for fathers and sons. A father needs to keep in mind that this is all part of a boy becoming a man. However, as with the mother, the thought of letting go can be painful for the father. Therefore, the PROP can be of great help in marking the coming of age with a celebration of the boy's life. It helps make the passage easier for the father, not just the boy.

Grandparents

'Much of that chance or incidental mingling has ended... grandfathers live away from grandchildren and many boys experience only the companionship of other boys who, from the point of view of initiators, know nothing at all.'

Robert Bly[59]

When his first grandchild was born, my father said: 'If I knew how great grandchildren were, I would have had them first.' Grandparents can have a special role to play in the raising of the young. They can bring a perspective, a history, accrued wisdom and can look at the big picture rather than worry about the small things that so often grip the attention of parents.

Apart from my parents, the greatest influence on my life has been my maternal grandmother. She lived a full life and died at the age of ninety-six while I was writing this book. She had five daughters and four of them gave her eighteen grandchildren between them. They in turn gave her thirty-two great-grandchildren, who had produced four great-great-grandchildren by the time she died. In total, in her lifetime there were fifty-nine descendants spread over four generations.

She experienced pretty well everything that life could throw at her – death, new life, healing, riches and poverty. The wisdom she passed on to me, I am now seeking to pass on to my sons. She relished life and celebrated the arrival of each day as a gift. I spent many happy hours with her, alongside riverbanks, in her van or exploring beaches, eating fresh oysters and clams. Hardly was there a conversation where she did not pass insights on to me. When Ryan was a toddler, she was already a great-grandmother several times over and I learned something from her. She was in our front garden picking fruit off a tree and Ryan was frolicking in the dirt at our feet. I was packing the car at the time and I called, 'Grandma, keep an eye on Ryan for me, he may try to eat the dirt.' She never glanced my way or Ryan's but as I disappeared into the house, I heard her quietly mumble, 'A little dirt never hurt anyone.' It stopped me in my tracks and I took note of practical wisdom.

Grandparents have a way of seeing the larger picture. They do not tend to worry about the small things and can bring a good dose of common sense to not only the boy but also his parents. However, she was the only grandparent I had. Her husband, my mother's step-father, was largely a good man, but interested more in his biological grandchildren than my sister, my brother and me. My paternal grandfather died when my father was just three, and my paternal grandmother died when I was nine. I recall my sister accusing me of being uncaring because I did not cry at her funeral. She was largely a stranger to me, as we lived a long way away and did not visit that much. While I did feel some emotion at her graveside, I did not feel a sense of loss.

A parent told me the other day that his grandparents were couch potatoes. Whenever he went to their house, they simply put the TV on for the evening and 'stuffed their faces.' This is sad, not just because it happens, but because it appears that many grandparents simply abandon their duty and privilege of helping bring up the young. There may be many causes for this, including distance. Some grandparents may actually feel their involvement is unwanted and viewed as interference by the child's parents. For the sake of our children, older people need to be active and visible. I recognise that it may not be possible for the biological grandparents to be involved. They may have died or live too far away. However, there may be older people in a family's net-work that are available, suitable and eager to be involved in the life of the family. In this age of email and the internet, there is no excuse for those grandparents who live a long way away not to communicate with their grandchildren – and vice versa. We live in Japan: nevertheless, we receive regular emails from both sets of grandparents, and both boys have added their grand-mother to their MSN chat 'buddies' list.

Mackenzie's mini-PROP at the age of ten began with breakfast with his two grandfathers. I watched Mac as he listened, not always understanding, yet imbibing something of their souls into his. The two grandfathers enjoyed telling their tales, their eyes at times fading into the distant shores of their memories. The two men are old friends and their stories often involved the other. There was a lively and loving spark between them and my son witnessed two older men relating to each other in a deeply transparent way. Later, in private, Mac and I talked about the breakfast experience. It turned out that he had understood a great deal but, more importantly, he had learned about matters of the heart as well. He had witnessed a mature male friendship and observed the results of true loyalty existing between old mates.

Grandfathers and older men should stand shoulder to shoulder with fathers and younger men in welcoming boys into manhood. This will teach the boy the importance of the generations and the male community. Shortly after Mac's mini-PROP, we made a journey to my grandmother. It was the last time I saw her before she passed away. Mac did not talk with her much; he simply stood in the tiny flat with his eyes glued to her as she talked with my mother and me. After cremation, she wished to have her ashes spread on the Pacific Ocean. We were unable to attend the funeral, but we did have our own memorial service for her in Japan, on the beach facing the Pacific. Both our boys participated as we paid tribute to a woman who had taught us all so much.

My Grandma

Woman stands in noble grey
Wearing dignity only years can buy
A smile betrays a private joy

Each day is a gift, she taught
Not with words spoken, rather
With eager joy that reached deep

I recalled the grand tree
A canopy of love
Over the family home

And a van freckled with flowers
Host to exquisite conversation
Causing curiosity to rise

Her ageing frame was home to a wise heart
Our matriarch, a veteran of life's storms
Celebrating the propulsion of Life

Eyes weary from a century of observation
Close when speaking of life's treasures
Yet twinkle with the knowledge of things unseen

The pain of a daughter lost
Could not suppress the fountain of joy

With moist eyes I witnessed
Multiple generations in solidarity
A family's continuum of life and joy

Light recently returned,
Brightened the visage
That greets the gift of each day

I watched her towering soul
Face life's uneven horizon
Gushing from a life fully lived

And the expanse of eternity

Then she was gone.
Finally reunited with all
That had gone before.

Written after seeing my grandmother for the last
time.

And all the rest: aunts, uncles, older cousins, close friends of the family

An inherent feature of the ideal nuclear family that emerged in the 1950s was an emphasis on the future at the expense of the past. This is rooted in a linear view of time and the notion that we must make the future better than the past. There is nothing wrong with wanting the best for our children, but we must be careful that we do not diminish the past and the role of those who have gone before. Throughout Scripture, we notice an emphasis on clans, nations, families and history. God is the Creator of all time and therefore we should affirm and celebrate the past as well as the future. In addition to providing shelter and food, families provide children with values, history and models of behaviour.

One man I spoke to recently, Robert Roche[60], told me of the role that his uncle and great uncle played in his becoming a man. When Robert was thirteen, he was unwittingly involved with a family ritual that all the male cousins before had gone through. There were twenty-seven cousins in all and he was number sixteen in line. The family ritual had become a well-established one and when he started to work for one of the family owned construction companies, there were still several cousins working on the site. His uncle Joe owned a company which largely did masonry work. Soon after turning thirteen, his mother took him to visit Uncle Joe. At first, Robert thought he was there just for a short visit, and while his mother and uncle were talking, his great Uncle Ted came by and gave him a job 'running the smoother over the mortar between newly laid bricks.' An hour or so later, Robert realized his mother had left and his uncle told him she would be back later and that he should keep working. He found out, that evening, that construction sites would be where he would spend his time on weekends, holidays and summers up to and during his college education. Robert told me in our interview, 'I was thrown into the sea of men. It was my rite of passage.' Robert's rite went on for several years. Every day, Robert would ride to work with his Great Uncle Ted, who was the master mason. Robert was mentored by his great uncle and by the other men on the site. Robert is not entirely sure why he ended up working for his Uncle Joe and not in one of the companies owned by other family members. He figures that Uncle Joe 'drew the short straw' and that his Great Uncle Ted 'paid the price.' 'I benefited from the input of not only my father but other men too', Robert told me. Robert eventually became a lawyer but opted for business over law. He runs his own successful company today and often reflects on the lessons he learned working alongside his uncles.

One of my uncles fought in the Second World War. I have learned a lot from him, not so much as a mentor but more as a role model. He is a tall strong man and has farmed all his life, and, like my grandfather and other relatives, has been involved in politics. I grew up in awe of my uncle's quiet dignity. He is a tender man who cares about people but also a strong, determined, confident man.

I learned more of what shaped him when I was his driver the summer he returned to Europe for the first time since the war. For ten days, I drove him along the route that he travelled near the end of the war. Starting at Dieppe, we eventually arrived in Holland and the canal that he had crossed, only to be trapped for several hours in the low grass, avoiding the crossfire. I followed him at a distance as we walked through graveyards searching for the graves of fallen comrades and watched him kneel and weep as he remembered. I had never thought about war much, but Uncle George talked to me about it at length on the journey. He had lived with the memories. It made me wish I had known him better earlier in my life. He had fought for the basic principles of freedom and liberty. On the fiftieth anniversary of the Allied victory, my sons and I phoned Uncle George and asked him where he was on VE day and what he felt when he heard the news. My sons listened intently as he told them the details. Later, in my own experiences in Bosnia, as an occasional visitor to the war-torn town of Mostar, the sound of gunfire helped me appreciate the horror of war, and bravery of people like my uncle.

Whether it is mother, father, aunt or uncle, grandparents or close friends of the family, the extended family has a significant role to play in the lives of boys and at their coming of age ceremonies. They need to know that their families, nuclear and extended, have witnessed and affirm their passage into adulthood. Boys need more than their peers to grow up. They need the company of caring, responsible adults.

'When adolescent boys spend most of their time with adult men at work and during leisure hours, anti-social behaviour is absent. When boys spend most of their time in peer groups, the level of anti-social behaviour is significantly elevated.'[61]

 **Key
Points**

- A boy need never separate from his mother. The PROP should mark the time when their relationship changes into friendship and interdependence
- Only men can welcome boys into manhood. If they do not, the boy will lack a certainty in his soul that he is truly grown up
- Grandparents can bring calm to a boy, by seeing the big picture and not necessarily worrying about the small things in life
- A boy needs to have many adults involved in his life. The extended family is a good starting point to find them.

Summary

Boys need the close involvement of mother and father figures and they benefit greatly from the active involvement of caring adults.

Tips and Ideas

- As a prelude to a mini-PROP or the main PROP of late teens, a mother and son could spend a night on the town or have a weekend retreat. This would provide an opportunity for a mother to speak with her son about life, women and the need for the boy to have a healthy and respectful view of everyone, particularly those who are different to himself.

- A father could involve other men in his son's mini-PROPs or the main PROP. The men could form a corridor at the end of the ceremony, symbolising the approval and affirmation of older men of the boy's life and passage.

- As part of a mini-PROP a boy could make a video of his family's history, interviewing grandparents and great-grandparents, if they are still alive.

- Phone an uncle or grandparent of your son and arrange an evening out together to discuss your son's life and possible mini-PROPs or PROPs that would be possible.

Engage the church

We live in an age when the extended family is not always available or supportive. Grandparents, aunts, uncles and cousins may live quite a distance away and be neither interested nor able to be involved in helping our children grow up. This reality of the twenty-first century family need not be an obstacle in bringing up healthy mature young people, if the local church is present and active. Keith Bozman is a father and a businessperson who started attending church five years ago. He wrote to me saying how grateful he is for the investment the church has made in his teenage sons.

It has been a real blessing to have both our boys surrounded by men and women (who lead the youth) who are straight arrows or who have fallen but have been able to share this with the youth in a positive light. I think young people look hard at their parents' lives and the people their family associates with and somehow discern what is right, acceptable or wrong. If you surround your family with good people, there is a better chance that your sons will understand right from wrong. This is not to say they will make the right decisions in every situation but it gives them a firm foundation. This all goes back to the notion that a community or church raises our children.

As someone who was brought up in the church, Keith's comments reminded me of the privilege it is to belong to a supportive faith community, something I have often taken for granted. The church can be a great support to families who are members but it should also reach out to boys and their families who are outside the church. It has a leading role to play in helping boys become men and can serve the community by inviting families with boys to participate in activities for boys and their parents and mentors. Camps, mission trips, and annual or bi-annual 'Coming of Age Ceremonies' could be a great means of outreach and service.

Community of faith

The church has three things to contribute to a successful PROP. The first is to emphasise to the boy the communal aspect of faith. The church is a community of faith. Dr Scott Peck, who wrote the best-seller *The Road Less Travelled*, brings an interesting perspective to the issue of community. He and his wife are the founders of an organisation that seeks to foster community values. He links the issue of personal peace with integrity within the community. He wrote 'Inner peace is a derivative of integrity, and the subject of integrity brings us back to community.'[62] It is a great insight. If we want our children to enjoy wholeness as adults, we need to nurture within them a state of inner peace. This peace is achieved by being at peace with others. What better community in which to discover this peace than the church family.

However, the influence of the community goes beyond the subjective, it actually works itself out in practice.

One of the many practical ways the church can help children is by providing support to lone parent families. Sadly, because of our idealisation of the nuclear family, many lone parents feel substandard and disadvantaged in bringing up children. This is unfortunate and need not be the case. I have observed many children brought up by lone parents who become responsible adults, while some children brought up in a two-parent family are immature adults. The reason? There may be many, but one may be that lone parents are more likely to recognise the need for help in the nurturing of their children and therefore they do reach out to allow and welcome caring and trustworthy adults to be involved. Whether it is as a support to lone parents or families where both parents live at home, the church can be of great help in extending a family's support network. The church as a community of faith has much to offer in teaching life skills and spiritual guidance.

Liturgy and symbols

'Rituals bind a community together, and also bind the individuals to the community.'
Kathleen Norris writing in *The Cloister Walk*[63]

The church also offers rich traditions in rituals, ceremonies, symbols and liturgies. No matter what our church tradition may be, we have centuries of practices that can be drawn on to bring the spiritual value of a PROP to the fore.

For example, Phil Wall, a former member of the London Police Riot Squad, leader in the Salvation Army and now popular speaker and consultant, told me of a mini-PROP in the Salvation Army where children are appointed as Junior Officers from seven upwards. Phil says that the 'idea was to capture kids at an early age around the vision of the gospel and give them actual roles in leading the church.' Phil admits that the practice may need a makeover: 'Junior Jedis or something' but believes the concept to be of timeless value.

Young people in western cultures have no function other than to consume. The emotional jump between not being needed and not being wanted is a very small one indeed – hence I believe a major 'rite of passage' for young men is for them to have a meaningful role/function that is recognised and affirmed within the church, and I do not mean taking up the collection/sitting on some toothless 'youf committee'.[64]

A mini-PROP in the Salvation Army

The Helper Year: to introduce ten year olds to leadership.

Duties of a Helper

To befriend one or two children in the five–nine age group, fulfilling the following expectations:
- helping their children in the activities of the structured session
- praying together with their children during the structured session
- phoning their children weekly to hear how their week is going and to gain prayer information
- praying daily at home for their children
- sending a birthday card to their children

- informing a leader if they are concerned in any way about their children
- to set a positive example in the group
- to help tidy the classroom at the end of the session.

Aims of a Helper Year

- to promote strong, spiritual growth in the ten year olds
- to develop a pastoral awareness in each of the children and to provide opportunities to exercise this awareness
- to encourage a regular prayer life on behalf of others
- to promote a sense of responsibility within the kids
- to excite the children about how God can use them now and not just in the future.

Most of us are familiar with the practice of confirmation which could be part of a mini-PROP. It involves the teaching of the faith and many churches offer a retreat before hand. The course culminates with the young person standing before a church leader (i.e. a Bishop) and a conversation going something like this:

Bishop: Do you reject the devil and all rebellion against God?
You: I reject them.
Bishop: Do you renounce the deceit and corruption of evil?
You: I renounce them.
Bishop: Do you turn to Christ as Saviour?
You: I turn to Christ.
Bishop: Do you submit to Christ as Lord?
You: I submit to Christ.

Bishop: Do you come to Christ, the way, the truth and the life?
You: I come to Christ.[65]

Some church streams have a tradition of giving a middle name at the confirmation. Some churches give the name of a saint, while others use biblical names. Other churches affirm the boy's legal name on the birth certificate and stress the meaning of it. There is power in a name. When I was in my late teens, I was given a St Christopher's Medal and when it was presented I was described as a David from the Old Testament. Even as I write, I feel inspired afresh by the attributes of St Christopher and David.

Confirmation in and of itself is not enough to be a rite of passage. It can serve as a key component in a PROP that also has other aspects that meet the three-fold criteria of a puberty rite of passage. Eric Delve explained how confirmation has become a sort of rite of passage but that this should not be the case. He wrote to me:

> Here at St Luke's, as in many parts of the Church of England, it is possible for Confirmation to have the same kind of significance. However, this is not what it was intended for, any more than Baptism was intended to be a puberty rite of passage. You have, therefore, set me thinking about whether we need to create some kind of ritual, both for men and women, in which we celebrate the fact that they've passed into adulthood.

I agree. Churches, no matter their denomination, have liturgies or practices in their historical repertoire that could form part of a PROP but there is a need for more. While writing this book, it has been difficult for me to find churches that have some form of PROP. I have canvassed widely, casting my net of inquiry to Anglicans, Methodists, Baptists, Pentecostals and the New Churches. While ideas have been in short supply, all have agreed that there is a vacuum and a need for innovation.

An obvious idea would be to have an annual 'coming of age ceremony' or graduation service. The Americans have a lovely term for their high school graduation event, a 'commencement ceremony'. Perhaps churches could do something similar. A church could easily organise such an event. It could have a formal as well as an informal element. It should follow a time of testing, which could include school exams and could be the culmination of a full PROP experience. Whether it marks graduation from high school, college or following a gap year, the church could help the young adult and their family celebrate the commencement of a new chapter of life as each of the young people are prayed for and the entire peer group is inducted into adulthood.

Will Bisset, a former RAF officer, a father and an active member of an Anglican church, thinks that the gateway to the church could be used as the central symbol and theme for a PROP. He suggests the following:

> Perhaps use the symbolism of the gateway (or use church doors?) and stress that there is also no turning back! It might even be appropriate here for the parents to be involved; they stay on one side of the gate or door, whilst the 'new' adults pass through the door symbolising that their parents' responsibilities for them are ended; that the children have become adults and are now responsible for themselves.

Will's idea of the gateway is excellent. Here is a possible order of service for a coming of age ceremony for boys and girls:

1 The congregation form a corridor outside the gate or doors of the church and family, mentors, and other key adults gather inside the gate.
2 Recruit or form a brass band to play something inspiring, such as Elgar's 'Pomp and Circumstance' as they lead a procession through the corridor.
3 Invite a politician, dignitary or local celebrity to bring a short (five minutes and no more!) speech of inspiration.
4 Each young person has their name called and, one by one, they walk through the crowd of people and pass through the gateway. Whilst they are walking, an outline of their life is read including their stated plans for the next phase of their life.
5 Once all the young people have walked through the gate, the ceremony could move indoors where they are invited to place something on the altar that is symbolic of their childhood. It could be a photograph, a childhood toy, or even a duvet! A public prayer of thanksgiving for their childhood years follows this act.
6 A PowerPoint or video presentation could follow that is a record of the adventure element of the PROP that has preceded the ceremony. If it was a gap year, the young person may want to tell in their own words what the year meant to them.
7 The men of the church and the families could lay their hands on the young people and pray for them, affirming their destiny as men and women.
8 The procession could then move onto the church hall for a welcome party.

Love...

The church not only is a liturgical community but should be a loving one too! Love is a commodity the church should have in abundance. 'Love' is the most sung about and romanticised of human attributes: it is also the most daring of values to live by. Without love, Christianity is simply a rigid set of dogmas. However, when people practise love as Jesus did, the collective faith of the church brings light and lift to individuals, families and whole communities. Boys need to be soaked in this kind of love. They need to be recipients of the loving service of the church and be the frequent recipient of words of grace and encouragement. Dr Pollack, in his seminal work on boys, said: 'Boys are never hurt by too much love.'[66] He is right. Paradoxically, it can hurt to love. Adults take a great risk in loving children, for it leaves us vulnerable to the choices our young people make. If we did not care, we would not be bothered. It is the fact we love so much that often means we feel exhausted. The rewards are great for boys, families, churches and communities. PROPs soaked in love can liberate a boy into his future with an emotional confidence and spiritual sustenance. If we are not prepared to take the risk of loving, we are opting for control and power rather than release and liberty.

The church has so much to offer boys in helping them become men, but we need to do more. The practices of having the whole congregation stand at baby dedications or when witnessing a teenager's confirmation are good but not enough. The church could lead the way for organising PROPs for entire peer groups in the church and the community. Responsible adults could be designated to plan, pray and participate in PROPs. The church can provide surrogate mothers, fathers, grand-parents etc. When I worked for British Youth for Christ, I was impressed by a practice that our staff in our one-year teams' programme had implemented. They assigned an 'angel' to each recruit who would do things anonymously for the student during their year of training. Leaving cards, a gift of money, a written prayer helped boost the students' sense that they were not alone. I like the concept of angels and who is better placed to assign angels to young people than the church? There is no need to keep it secret though. Young people will benefit from knowing that there are designated adults who are trustworthy and approved to be available to them for counsel and support and who will be present as a witness at their coming of age ceremony.

Summary

The church has a strategic role to play in offering support to families in raising boys generally and drawing on its rich traditions to organising meaningful mini-PROPs and PROPs.

 Key Points

- The church as a community of faith can teach life skills and provide spiritual guidance
- Every church has its own culture and set of traditions; a rich treasure of liturgy, ritual and symbolism that can be drawn from
- The most obvious feature that the church expresses (or should express) is love. Boys can never get too much love and therefore church should be a safe and nurturing place.

Tips and Ideas

- Organise adventure weekends for sons and fathers.
- Encourage gap years and mission trips.

- Integrate confirmation classes into mini-PROPs in the early teens and have a renewal of confirmation vows in the final PROP. The confirmation is not a rite of passage into adulthood, but it is important in the building of belief, an important aspect of a PROP. For those who have entered the church later, the confirmation process can run parallel to the PROP, each re-enforcing the other.

- The use of Alpha could be integrated into a PROP, but not the Youth Alpha. You want to signify to the young person that they have become an adult and can and should face adult issues in an adult manner. While we do not confuse becoming Christians with becoming men, the use of a catechism can help a boy grow intellectually, in the knowledge of values and be triggered spiritually, all of which is necessary for a child to mature and become a whole person as an adult.

- Provide a 'Blessing Ceremony' for any or all of the following: graduation from secondary school and/or university, entering the workplace, before or after a gap year – or both.

- Organise a special ceremony for those who have received their driver's licence. Someone could give a talk from the world of motor sports and prayers of protection offered for the new drivers – and the pedestrians and other drivers they will meet on the road!

- Put the book down now and pray for insight as to how your church could actively help boys become men. Then call some other parents and a church leader to talk about it.

Conclusion: Enjoy the journey!

'Life is a journey.' How many times have you heard that well-worn phrase? I do not know when or where I heard it for the first time, but I recall my head nodding involuntarily in agreement, gratefully welcoming four words that seemed to articulate something I knew intuitively. However, after the umpteenth exposure, the words became stored in the place in my brain reserved for phrases that were 'once enlightening but are now dulled through over-use.' It is rather like 'God is love,' the famous biblical statement that appears on countless day-glo signs seeking to contrast themselves from worn, red-brick or grey-stone church buildings throughout the UK, and on what the Americans call bumper stickers. Reduced to jargon, the phrase, if it touches the reader or listener at all, merely triggers an inner, imperceptible yawn.

Yet despite the erosion of its power, the statement 'Life is a journey', like 'God is love', is true. Let us imagine we are listening to it for the first time. Say the words slowly to yourself, allowing the truth of them to seep deeply. Each separate word deserves thoughtful meditation, but, when combined, there is a synergy bringing insight and revelation. We have the privilege of watching and participating on our boys' journey through into manhood. We are not mere spectators but we have a responsibility to be involved with them sometimes as guides and counsellors and other times cheerleaders.

The journey of life is a challenge for boys today and they need our help. There are no guarantees in bringing up children. The methods we use and the resources we need must be diverse and multifaceted. As on any journey, a course must be plotted and occasionally the traveller must pause to ascertain where they are and to choose a way forward. A PROP provides such an opportunity. Although it may not be feasible in the times we live to allow a twelve year boy to embark on a non-stop, unescorted two hundred mile bike ride as Eric Delve did, it is possible to provide purposeful adventures and ceremonies. Like Eric, boys need an emotional marker to be laid down, in order to grow up more confident that they can not only survive but also succeed in an adult world. My thirty-five mile walk and later my gap year in Mexico were for me what Eric's monumental bike ride was for him. I must now allow my boys the same opportunities that Eric's and my parents allowed us.

The world has changed, the times are complex but one thing is for sure – our boys need our help. Life is full of accidental mini-PROPs but our boys will be helped to mature if families and churches think creatively and courageously in how to provide 'markers' helping boys successfully make the passage to manhood. It is time to get back to basics and learn from time proven practices like PROPs. Boys want to grow up and, if their families do not help them, they will devise their own means to prove themselves men.

As on every long journey, sometimes as parents we get lost, make mistakes and despair at our apparent stupidity. A few days ago, I muttered to myself, 'I am not cut out for this.' I was in the bath, feeling sorry for myself after a gruelling weekend as a parent. On the verge of tears, I found myself wishing I did not love my children so much.

It is not always easy, is it? We can feel we are doing all the right things for our children in terms of input, guidance and providing meaningful experiences but enough is never enough – despite our children feeling that enough is in fact too much. I have written this book in a deliberately upbeat manner. I believe that the adventure of bringing up children is dangerous but it is also full of promise and opportunity. We have every reason to be hopeful. However, the obvious fact is that our children will fail us, we will fail our children and if we do not embrace the inevitability of disappointment, we will be rudely awakened to its reality someday soon! Yet even in failure we can find promise. My son, Mackenzie, reminded me of this recently.

Mackenzie loves to draw strip cartoons. His stories are brilliantly insightful and funny (I suppose I have a bias). They feature an ant called Spud who, through everyday events, learns lessons about himself and his family. One day, in the presence of two women Kande and I were visiting, Mackenzie was creating another Spud cartoon strip. Soon their attention turned to Mackenzie and his drawing. They were intrigued that Mackenzie was drawing in ink and not pencil. One of the women asked Mackenzie, 'What do you do if you make a mistake?' Without looking up, he replied, 'I just make something out of it.' The women's eyes opened wide and jaws dropped. One of them muttered 'out of the mouths of babes…'

I have referred to our two sons Ryan and Mackenzie but in fact, as I have already written, we have three sons.

Our firstborn, Luke, does not live with us. He is in heaven. He only lived on earth for three days before death snatched him away. You can imagine our sadness. Many people helped us during that time including the Black Country man I mentioned earlier in the book and our dear friend and Baptist minister, Stephen Gaukroger. Stephen spoke at the service that followed Luke's cremation and told the story of a famous a painter who had a five year old son. I recollect the modern day parable going something like this: One day, the painter had a fresh canvas on his easel waiting to become a masterpiece. The five year old son, angry with his father for some reason, hurled a fist full of black paint into the centre of the pristine canvas, leaving a horrible ugly black splotch. The father stood back in surprise and amazement and told his son to sit down as punishment. The father then began mixing paints on his palette and proceeded to paint. He did not try to scrub the black paint off – thereby erasing the ugliness – but rather he used the mark as a backdrop and painted a masterpiece.

I have often reflected on the story. Whether it the result of our own failure, rebellion or sin, or we are suddenly struck with one of life's mysterious moments of darkness and we are groping for some light and struggling to get answers to troubling questions, God the great painter does the same for us. He turns what was meant for evil into good. Our lives are drawn in ink and therefore nothing can be erased from the portraits of our lives. The good news is that God can convert our errors into his advantages.

As we have already seen, one of the hardest things to do as a parent is to allow our children to make decisions knowing that their choices, often made on the spur of the moment, can dramatically alter their lives and those around them. So what do we do when our kids disappoint us? Do we blame it on the devil, their genes, their peers, the media, or ourselves? I have seen the children of well rounded caring parents turn out badly, and the children of a dysfunctional home turn out brilliantly. It does come down to the choices our kids make. So here is some advice.

- Accept the inevitability of disappointment. Life is not a series of successes. The wise adult learns from their mistakes.
- Always assure your child of your love no matter what they have done. Once the assurance has been given, then talk about the discipline and lessons learned.
- Learn to forgive yourself and embrace the promise in Scripture that 'all things work together for good'. Remember that the only criteria is that we seek first his Kingdom. In other words, if our lives are predisposed towards living out Christian values we can have confidence in those times when mistakes are made that we can find forgiveness and somehow God can convert bad into good.

In the journey of life, there will be many crises. However, fear of crisis should not prevent us from giving our boys our all. For although there are dangers inherent in every crisis, there are also great opportunities. As parents and involved adults, we need to find the balance between being participants and being spectators. If we err towards one more than the other, let it be towards involvement. Our job is not to entertain our kids with lots of 'cool' experiences, but to blend purposeful adventure with the teaching of beliefs and meaningful ceremonies that celebrate the boy becoming a man. Watching our children grow up is an adventure. They will pass through several phases on their journey to adulthood, each needing a mini-PROP of some sort. When the day finally arrives for the boy to become a man, we can stand proudly by, witnessing their passage into adulthood, knowing that despite failures along the way, our investment in the boy's journey to adulthood has been worth it.

DIY kit

It is over to you now. This section of the book is to start you off planning mini-PROPs and PROPs for the budding men in your life. It need not be restricted to boys, though. If you have been inspired to do the same for the girls, then why wait. Start planning! The children of today and the adults of tomorrow will enjoy the rewards of your investment.

Step one: Write your own A-Z guide

Every young person is different. They have unique needs, traits and circumstances. Their very existence challenges any 'How To' manual in how to raise them. As parents, we have our share of grief and gratitude bringing up our children but we all have insights that can benefit others. I asked a group of adults at Spring Harvest to write down twenty-six words in alphabetical order that came to mind when thinking of boys and what they need. This section contains their responses. The list is nowhere near complete. It needs your contributions. So, please read this section with a pen in hand. If a word that appears finds resonance, then underline or circle it and then write down any new ones that come to mind. The exercise will help you focus on the needs and nature of boys and hopefully spark creative thoughts and ideas on how to help them grow up to be men. If you are doing this exercise with girls in mind, then simply add another column or use a different sheet. It would be an interesting exercise to cross-reference the two, in order to discover where there is overlap and contrast. Who knows, one of you may feel inspired to write a book for girls. I have offered little comment through the list, but have occasionally placed a word in a box when I felt I wanted to add something. Have fun! Some words were mentioned more than others and so the most popular words appear in bold at the beginning of the list and the rest are in random order.

A
Affirmation
Adventure, ambition, acceptance, achievement, advice, answers, acknowledgement, activity, assistance

> **My Choice: Attitude.** It is not our aptitude that determines our altitude in life, but our attitudes that affect us most. Boys need admonishment on how to do 'an attitude check' when their behaviour is bad. Attitude checks must begin very early in the child's life. When attitudes are wrong, life is lived on the wrong footing. Desires and habits take a downward spiral. Brooding and anti-social behaviour becomes evident.

B
Belonging

Bravado, Bible, belief, boisterousness, balance, body language, boredom NOT, battles to fight, brotherly love, brash, boundaries

C
Confidence and choices

Compassion, courage, community, consultation, conversation, challenges, care, creativity, confusion, conflict

> **My Choice: Cave.** One Spring Harvest guest wrote 'cave' as something boys need. The word made me think. It's true. Boys need a private place, a zone where they can mellow out, reflect and work things through in their minds and souls. It may not be a physical place, but a mental, emotional and spiritual state of mind.

D
Determination

Discouragement, discipline, direction, domestication, daddy, drive, doubt, deep

> **My Choice: Dignity.** Without it a boy is a wimp. It is his personhood. He receives dignity through consistent and caring discipline and constant affirmation.

E
Encouragement and exercise

Energy, emotions, examples, experience, excitement, empowerment, enjoyment, eating, extended family, entertaining

F
Friends and fathers
Fun, freedom, faith, fairness, falling, fear, food, fellowship, football, family

G
Guidance and girls
Grandparents, growth, grief, God, guts, greatness, gratitude, gifts, goals

H
Hope
Holiness, hugs, height, horizons, homes, help, homework, honesty, hormones, high standards, healing, happiness, humour, humility, handsome

My Choice: Heroes. Every boy needs several.

I
Independence
Ideals, intelligence, imagination, instruction, inclusion, integration, interests, ideals, integrity, intimacy, initiative, intuition, injury

My Choice: Interaction with others promotes stimulation of ideas and growth of character.

J
Jokes
Joy, journeys, justice, Jesus, jest, job, jibe

K
Knowledge and kindness
Kinship, kicking a ball, kites

L
Love
Learning, life-style, life-skills, listened to, laughter, letting go, life, lonely

M
Mum
Mistakes, music, mess, money, maturity, models, mission, morality, meals together, memories, masculinity, mentors, muscles, men

N
Nurture
Noise, new, No, novelty, nature

O
Opportunities and openness
Outdoors, obstacles, outlook, ownership, old

> **My Choice: Opinions**: It is good to have your own! We can learn too, by listening to our boys' opinions.

P
Pocket money, praise and play
Peanut butter, pizza, prayer, purpose, personality, perseverance, potential, physical play, place, privacy, pressure, patience, pain, passion, peers, protection, parents, prizes, pubic hair

> **My Choice: Peers**. This is where healthy self-opinions come in handy. Being like everyone else doesn't make us unique.

Q
Quiet and questions
Quests, quality, IQ

> **My Choice: Quizzing**. One can learn much by quizzing the mind of a wise person. We need to encourage our boys to listen to the sage advice of others.

R
Rest and responsibility
Role models, rough and tumble, rest, recreation, reasons, roots, ritual, routine

> **My Choice: Respect** for others.

S
Space and sports
Skateboards, sleep, structure, security, safety, spirituality, stories, symbols, sharing, surprises, support, sex, sisters, stability, self-reliance, status, sayings, silliness

T
Time, teaching and trust
Talking, tolerance, training, testing, testosterone, tears, teachers, traditions, togetherness

U
Understanding
Untidiness, unconditional love, unity, universe, unusual

My Choice: Uniqueness. Daring to be different.

V
Values
Vocation, viewpoints, valued, vision, victory, volunteer work, vulnerability, vitality, vim

W
Wisdom and work
Water, washing, what is wrong, welcome, wrestling, worldview, worth

X
eXpression
eXcitement, x-ray vision, eXtended family, xylophone (eXpress creativity), eXercise, seX

My Choice: eXample. As parents we need to set an example to our boys and in turn we need to remind them that they also have a responsibility to the generation coming behind them.

Y
Yearning
Youthfulness, yes, yesterdays

Z
Zeal
Zoo, zzzzzzz's, zest

Step two: Telling the story

Write a life history of the boy or girl for whom you are wanting to plan a mini-PROP or a PROP. If you are not a parent, think of a nephew, a niece, a young person in your church etc. Tell their story through your eyes. Keep it to two or three paragraphs, but list the key moments of their growing up as you see it. This narrative will help you later when you meet with the child to discuss and organise their PROP.

Begin with their birth and end with their present. Then go on to a dream about their future or futures. There is some space here for you to jot your thoughts, but do get a clean piece of paper to finish it later.

Their Story:

Step three: Planning the PROP

Use the form below to outline the PROP. Feel free to make as many copies as you like. If my form is unhelpful, then design your own. Make sure you involve the child in the process. Take time, though, to make sure they understand what a rite of passage is and how it can help them grow up.

Name of child:
Age of child:

1

   a Is it to be a mini-PROP? If so what are the ages and milestones that you feel are important? For example: are they becoming an adolescent? Becoming a teenager? Moving schools? Being confirmed?

   b If it is the main PROP, what other events are related that can be incorporated? For example: getting a driver's licence? Graduation from school? Voting for the first time?

2 Theme:

---

3 Possible dates and duration:

4 How will I incorporate the three elements of a PROP?

   a Adventure with purpose:

   b Building belief:

   c Ceremony and celebration

5 Once you have answered these questions, you can add further variety by:

   a Cross-referencing what you wrote with the concepts of risk, ritual and recognition.

   b How will the child be challenged and taken beyond their comfort zone?

   c Is there time for contemplation and an emphasis on spirituality?

   d How will you involve the church and/or the extended family?

e What privileges and responsibilities will be bestowed?

f What symbols, nicknames, metaphors can be used in the final ceremony?

6 What resources and budget might be needed?

7 What does your child think?

Step four: Get on with it

Well... go ahead then!

Endnotes

[1] Barclay Mcbain, 'The Gender Gap that threatens to become a chasm', *Glasgow Herald*, 17 September, 1996, 16

[2] Sommers, C., *The War Against Boys* (London: Simon & Schuster, 2000), 38

[3] Barclay Mcbain, 15

[4] 'Tomorrow's Second Sex', *The Economist*, 28 September, 1996, 23

[5] 1 Corinthians 13:11

[6] Sommers C., 180-181

[7] Morris, E., MP, Labour Conference, 'Boys will be Boys?: Closing the Gender Gap' (London: Labour Party, November 1996), 10

[8] Sommers, C., 210

[9] Bly, R., *Iron John: A Book About Men* (New York; Addison Wesley, 1990), 234

[10] Sommers C., 153

[11] Peck, S., *In Search Of Stones* (Simon & Schuster, 1995), 150

[12] Sheehy, G., *Understanding Men's Passages* (New York: Random House, 1998), 55

[13] van Gennep, A., *Rites of Passage* (Chicago; University of Chicago Press, 1960)

[14] Pollack, W., *Real Boys* (New York; Henry Holt and Company, 1998), 46

[15] Molitor, B., *A Boy's Passage: Celebrating Your Son's Journey to Maturity* (Colorado Springs: Harold Shaw Pub, 2001), 2

[16] Cole M. and Cole S., *The Development of Children* (California; Worth Publishers, 2001), 587

[17] Cole 687

[18] Peterson E., *The Message* (Colorado Springs: NavPress, 1993), 123–124

[19] Hendrix, H., and H. Hunt, *Giving the Love that Heals: A Guide for Parents* (New York; Pocket Books, 1997), 289

[20] Bly, 38

[21] Biddulph, S., *Raising Boys* (HarperCollins, 1998), 203

[22] Taken from an essay written by an eleven year old on rites of passage.

[23] Cole, 624

[24] Cole, 624

[25] Cole, 625 (The quote is from a paper called, 'Playing with Desire: An interpretative perspective on adolescent risk-taking' presented by C. Lightfoot in 1994)

[26] To find out more about Adventure Therapy search the internet. Sites abound in cyberspace.

[27] Bly, 33

[28] Boyd, S., Longwood W., Muesse M.W., *Redeeming Men* (Kentucky: Westminster John Knox Press, 1996), 194

[29] Rechtschaffen, S, *Time Shifting: Creating More Time to Enjoy Your Life* (New York: Doubleday, 1996), 159

[30] McCloughry, R., *Men and Masculinity: from power to love* (London: Hodder and Stoughton, 1992), 103

[31] Bly, 6

[32] Norris, K., *The Cloister Walk* (Oxford: Lion, 2000)

[33] Jackson, P,. and Delehanty, H., *Sacred Hoops: Spiritual Lessons of a Hardwood Warrior* (New York: Hyperion, 1995), 3

[34] McCloughry, 112

[35] Boyd, 190

[36] Eric Delve, the Vicar of Luke's Maidstone and Area Dean, told me this remarkable story when we were at Spring Harvest.

[37] For more on blogging go to www.blogspot.com. If you want to check out how a blog can be used, go to http://jonny-baker.blogspot.com, the blog of my friend Jonny Baker.

[38] Hebrews 11:6

[39] My first book, co-written with Catherine Butcher and published by Crossway, is named *Never Ending Adventure*. The phrase is attributed to John Wesley, who was once asked to define Christianity. His reported response inspired the title of our book.

[40] Biddulph, 23

[41] http://crystalinks.com/visionquest.html

[42] Pollack, 179

[43] Baldock, John., *The Elements of Christian Symbolism* (Element Books, Dorset 1990), 1

[44] Webber R., *Ancient-Future Faith: Rethinking Evangelicalism for a Post-modern World* (Grand Rapids: Baker, 1999), 107

[45] Jackson, 9

[46] Hendrix, 267

[47] Jackson, 21

[48] Foster, R.J., *Money, Sex & Power* (London: Hodder and Stoughton, 1985), Foster devotes a third of his book to the Biblical financial principles

[49] Bly, 29

[50] Biddulph, 4

[51] McCloughry, 107

[52] Koyama K., *Three Mile an Hour God* (London: SCM Press Ltd, 1979) This delightful book seems only to be available in second hand book shops in the UK

[53] Senator Hillary Clinton's speeches on this subject, when she was First Lady, placed this phrase in the national consciousness of America. Her remarks caused controversy and aroused the ire of many conservatives who believed that she was undermining the post war ideal of the nuclear family.

[54] Pollack, 173

[55] Pollack, 173

[56] Pollack, 173

[57] Pollack, 99

[58] Thompson, 35

[59] Bly, 15

[60] Robert Roche, who grew up in Chicago, runs a successful company in Japan.

[61] Cole, 624

[62] Peck, 261

[63] Norris, K., *The Cloister Walk* (Oxford: Lion, 2000)

[64] Phil Wall is a respected and experienced Christian leader who is now involved in working with the business community. You can find out more about him at www.bsignificant.com.

[65] Sent by Pete Broadbent, Bishop of Willesden and taken from *Common Worship*.

[66] Pollack, 137